*Tribute*

*To our fellow citizens
who were slaughtered in the
name of Jihad and "records of that
brutality had been totally
deleted from the official
books of History.*

## *Confession.*

The events mentioned in this book are more or less a century old and I did not witness any of them personally. Furthermore I am not a historian but I do present here what I learned from various authors. Unfortunately Modern History of India is not dependable because facts have been grossly distorted. I am presenting various factual although unpopular aspect of the reality which were intentionally been hidden or deleted for some unknown reason. You may kindly take this book as a compilation and in case of any dispute the author will not be responsible for that. Rather, such disputes may kindly be verified through the recommended literature or through Google search.

### *Dr. H. B. Singh*

# You need not stoop to conquer

It is necessary to study historical back -ground of any problem to find out the root cause – because only then, you can offer an effective management. The status of communal harmony today is that nation is struggling to wipe out the mark of defeat and invasion but Islamic leaders are struggling to retain them. There had been occasions when Muslim Mob did not allow the execution of the court order. Frankly there is an exercise of power between the two communities.

This situation is an outcome of all that have been done in the past, particularly during Gandhian age of British India and also in the secular India. You can find out that Mahatma Gandhi used the banner of "Hindu-Muslim-Unity" to cover his appeasement policy of Ali Brothers which caused eventually a Hindu Genocide. This field experience and also that gained during Kohat massacre added an impetus to Islamic up rise in British India and made them confident to plan some another calamity. They took 23 years after kohat massacre to change demography of Bengal and orchestrate the Great Killing of Calcutta. Appeasing hands of Mahatma Gandhi brought up Muslim League to the level of congress beyond which Jinna himself walked above the congress and took Pakistan away from India. Thus Islamic leader's today have a cause to think and act against Hindu.

Even the congress continued the tradition of appeasing Muslim and ignoring Hindu. This boosted Islamic leaders to take them above the ordinary Hindu of this country. Secular Parties did favor Islamic leadership even by misusing the government rule and penal code to favor them. Thus by the end of 2013 Islamic leadership had developed habit of relating them with the Mogul as ruler of this land. They developed a habit to encroach the civil and legal boundaries in India.

But the India Today is not that estate which was before 2013. The umbilical cord which was then - providing essential food and nutrition from the Government end is now been legated and severed. Besides, Muslim community at large will turn away from them in moments of crisis. The only thing that is required on the side of Nationalist is to remain united for the sake of dignity and dominance... and also to be consistent and persistent on persuading the issue of national integrity and complete liberty. The power of nationalism and patriotism can break through Alps even, these few hundreds of leadership are no barrier and this much you can take for granted that

*You need not stoop to conquer.*

*To*

*Little Masters of my family*
*Perth and Aakarsh,*
*my lovely Grand Sons*

# *I am not going*

to tell you the history (as I am not a historian) rather this book will tell you a story of Islamic up rise and Hindu Genocide in the name of Jihad exactly within the Gandhian Age of British India and during post independence secular India also.

The IT has changed the knowledge - almost about everything and that also substantially. The story in this book has its origin in the free-flow of uncensored information in the IT Age. Such information will give you a deeper eye into the evolving state of India. This story may make you to rethink about several events which transformed Hindusthan into India.

It may please be submitted here that every sincere and concerned reader may face questions like *(1)* *"why the reality of Mahatma Gandhi is found otherwise? (2) Why do scholars say as* ***"Publicity was taken as reality"*** in case of Mahatma Gandhi?

***Such disputes demand your serious concern to explore the matter towards truth.***

*xxxxxxxxxxxxxx*

*By the way* **"Have you heard of "**

**1. Mapilla Massacre?**
**2. Kohat Genocide?**
**3. Direct Action Day?**
**4. Noakhali Genocide?**
**5. Brahmin Genocide?**

**Most possibly you might have not!**

**However below mentioned particulars may kindly be referred**

1. "The Mapilla Rebellion, 1921" written by <u>Divan Bahadur C. Gopalan Nair,</u>
   1. Col. G. B. Singh – "Gandhi behind Mask of Divinity"- APR-2004, Promathew's Book.
   2. David Livingston – "The Untold Story of Gandhi and Theosophy"
   3. British Secret Service Agent Mahatma Gandhi http:// <u>www.reformation.org/british-secret-service-agent-mahatma-gandhi</u> html
   4. Nathuram Vinayak Godse and Gopal Vinayak Godse *"May it Please Your Honor" Surya Prakashan*
   5. David Collins – *"Gandhi was a British Agent who did great harm to India" – top judge – March 11 2015 mirror.co.uk/news/world news/Gandhi-agent-who did great -5316551*
   6. *Sergeant Major Gandhi was a British Secret Service Agent Himalayan Journal of Education and Literature, vol2-issue 4-AUG 31-2021*

# No Memorial

During British India people were being martyred in the independence movement (both militant and non violent) on the one hand and on the other people were been slaughtered by Jehadi Islamist. India does pay its gratitude to those who were martyred but not to those who were been slaughtered .... and this is because "that portion of history was totally erased" ........ and people really don't know about them. However *Islamic activists didn't forget to celebrate centenary of Mapilla Genocide ...... or victory of brutality on humanity.*

Fears None But God

BLiTZ

OPED

**Islamists celebrate Hindu genocide in India**

# Contents

# Chapter I

# Introduction

World's most ancient culture and civilization appeared in the Valley of Indus River somewhere about 5000 BC. This civilization was very much wealthy and had its own school of Philosophy called Sanatan Darshan. People of this civilization believed in non violent way of living but were expert in violent way of self defense and winning over the enemy. However for some unknown reason this civilization - though retained the philosophy and wealth but - lost the weapons and warrior like skill and thus became vulnerable to invasions. Grand period of invaded India may be discussed in following Ages.

***Islamic India:*** History wise Md. Bin Quasim was the first invader who invaded India in 711 AD. Furthermore right from Quasim to Aurangzeb there is a story of oppression of Hindu with a motto to establish an Islamic Estate. Islamic invaders converted Hindu forcefully, slaughtered those Hindu who denied, raped their women, played with children by sword, looted their property and the remaining was thrown into fire. To conclude the Islamic invaders and Mogul Empire ***intended to destroy the residents of this land, their culture and their religion and philosophy also, under the banner of jihad.***

***British India*** – with industrial revolution - turned capitalist primarily and now their motto was to develop Human Resources. They developed an education system which educated people to work for salary or consultation fee and provide benefit to the capitalist. Thus every Indian became either Employed or Self employed but not an entrepreneur. *The rational Hindu was thus converted to a consuming machine. Thus the industrial culture inflicted injury on religious aspect of culture and civilization which were* *more grievous than the Islamic barbarism although this poison was sweet and palatable.*

**Gandhian Age:** Mr. M. K. Gandhi appeared in the Indian politics about 100 years ago. He was a veteran of nonviolent passive resistance as it was advertised by Media before Mr. Gandhi got back from South Africa. *"Hindu Muslim Unity -- was the revised Indian edition of Ganddhian Philosophy"* and all through his life Mr. Gandhi advocated loudly for secularism. Mr. Gandhi was either grossly confused or he acted willfully in such a way that it became virtually difficult to say that whose side he was? This issue was appreciated widely by almost all the authors who evident from title of a book "will the real Gandhi stand up please?" published during Gandhian age of British India. It is really difficult to say that he was working for India, Muslim League or British Empire ?

**Secular India:** Endeavor of the secular state is that it will be illegal when you are Hindu. Before Mr. Gandhi and Nehru the congress basically was an association of or platform for all who were seeking independence but Gandhi and Nehru Hijacked this association to make a political party and now the essence of INC was that only congress is the association of Patriots. These two fellow – bagged sacrifices and services done for every non violent independent leader to their own credit and thus Nehru became as great as Lok Manya Tilak, Baal Gangadhar ....... Madan Mohan Malviyaa and every other political worker of Brittish India. The followers of Mr. Gandhi i.e. the INC constituted the Government in Independent India. But, let's begin long back in the Gandhian age. This secularism in fact widened the gap between Hindu and Muslim and then people and leaders got polarized toward their respective poles. Lay mans calculation is that once in the British India when general election were held on the declared issue of partition of India. Needless to say that INC was against it while Muslim League was in favor. The INC won the election with overwhelming majority while Muslim League has banged almost every seat in Muslim Dominated constituencies and provinces. The result of that election was very much speaking that Muslim voted for creation of Pakistan but on which ground it was taken (by the leaders) that *Hindu had voted for a secular Nation? Certainly this was not the mandate.* Furthermore, when separate land had been awarded to the Muslim fellows then why not the remaining piece of land was made Hindustan? Whether only 9% Muslim (census 1951) population did really qualify to prevent the creation of Hindu Country? Had the leadership been really concerned with even a single Muslim?

But unfortunately the reminiscences of all those three historical trends do still persist in our society and they are still alive and effective. Let's revise once again that these forces are:

1. Islam with sole intension to deprive this land off the Hindu and Hinduism
2. Capitalism to convert the Man power of India into Human Resource for the capitalistic system and destroying Hindu and Hinduism through economic reforms.
3. Secularism: This secularism was used by the government to appease Muslim and oppress Hindu in a legal way.

*Thus Communism became communalism in India and Hinduism was frustrated. When Hindu protested the up rise of Islam once again – Hindu terrorism was alleged in its own land and this is possible in India only.*

### Definite Agenda or Strategy

The ultimate motto of all the three historical forces stated above is to make India free of Hindu and Hinduism. It will not be an exaggeration if we say that communism has converted into communalism in India. This may become evident in following cases

1. **Brahmin Genocide in 1948:** Mahatma Gandhi was assassinated for some unknown reason - because submission of the accused was not published. Besides, medico legal practices were not adopted in case of Mahatma Gandhi's assassination. However the moment mahatma was declared to be assassinated a wave of massacre of maharastrian Brahmin spread at a very high speed and it took 8000 lives within 24 hours. .... Because N. R. Godse was a Brahmin but yet does it justify that every innocent Maharastrian Brahmin was to be slaughtered?. Furthermore, can the Governance be allowed to mourn the

assassination and at the same time ignore one massacre within Nation? *This is certainly illegal yet the estate makes a bold appeal to observe fraternity, communal harmony and peace!*

2. *Anti cow-slaughter agitation:* Anti cow slaughter movement was led by a Hindu saint swami Karpatri ji. This agitation was offering peaceful "dharna" before parliament of India in 1966. Total of 1,00,000 and even more were present in that crowd. Those were the days of Mrs. Gandhi and accordingly fire was opened on the crowd, several killed and then been thrown into Yamuna or cremated by Delhi police and also the press was threatened not to publish any news about this massacre. Naturally, event was not recorded in the books of History..... and the Government wants communal harmony to be maintained obviously by Hindu.

3. *Sah Bano case:* Sah bano was a divorcee Muslim lady. She refused to take compensation as per Shariat Kanoon and filed a case in court of law for maintenance permissible by Rules of

constitution of India. It took several years but ultimately an observation was made in favor of Sah bano on the ground that there is no mention of Sariat in cconstitution of India hence she is entitled to all the benefits and compensations according to the law of land.

**Now,** this case was neither in the support of any issue of national interest nor the order of Supreme Court was creating any sort of constitutional crisis .....But still then prime minister got a bill approved by parliament to quash the order of Supreme Court.

However such action of executive body of the nation using extraordinary judicature of parliament to quash the order of Supreme Court which was exactly in accordance with the constitution of India.

*Yet the state expects "fraternity and communal harmony" to be observed" by people........ Does it make any sense?*

## 4. Sikh Genocide of 1984

Sikh genocide initiated and spread to whole of the country. Here and there and everywhere. Sikh were been slaughtered. This was because of the fact that the person who has assassinated Mrs. Gandhi was a Sikh. However. This does not mean that every other Sikh must be slaughtered. But it was done in this manner and that also was sponsored by congress party itself.

5. *The Kashmir Files* is now open for everyone. This movie will become a documentary evidence and it will support our alleged shape of Islam – as stated above – is unchanged even today

The *above said events (No.1 to 5)* provide a record of violence in nonviolent nation of Mahatma Gandhi. How do you feel here?

## 6. *Hindu Genocide of Gandhian age:*

This book will discuss"*Hindu Genocide during Gandhian age of British India*" in a little detail and you may find it in following Chapters. However these chapters will tell you the story of a serial Genocide which claimed innocent lives en mass in recurrent manner and _this Hindu genocide will make you to think_

### "Whether Mr. Gandhi was really a Nonviolent Mahatma?

We will discuss this topic in a little detail in chapter 8 of this book. However – till then – let's evaluate the gravity of Genocide of _**"Hindu in their Homeland"**_.

However, book with name as "The Mapilla Rebellion, 1921" written by Diwan Bahadur C. Gopalan Nair, narrates how - even before the Mapilla massacre of Hindus in 1921 - intermittently, there were times when Muslims went into a frenzy and slaughtered Hindus. He writes how the Muslims would sometimes go into their "Hal Ilakam" (Religious frenzy) and not only slaughter Hindus but also desecrate their temples.

At that time, one Mr. TL Strange as the special commissioner in Malabar to understand what the cause of these frenzied episodes are. In an 1852 report, Mr. Strange wrote:

*"It is apparent that in no insistence can any outbreak or threat of outbreak that has risen be attributed to the oppression of tenants by landlords. A great clamor is now raised on this regard, prominently in the southern taluks visited by me, the Mapilla population seeking to throw the blame of these outbreaks upon the landlords by thus charging them with being the cause thereof. I have given the subject every attention and am convinced that though instances may and do arise of individual hardship of the tenant, the general character of the dealing of the Hindu landlords towards their tenant, whether Mapilla or Hindu, is mild, equitable and forbearing. I am further convinced that where stringent measures are taken, the conduct of the tenants is in the vast majority of cases, the cause thereof and that the Mapilla tenant, especially of the Taluks in the South Malabar, where the outbreaks have been so common are very prone to evade their*

*obligations and to resort to false and litigious pleas".*

He further said:

*"A 'feature that has been manifestly common to the whole of these affairs is that they have been one and all marked by the most decided fanaticism, and this, there can be no doubt, has 'furnished the true incentive to them. The Hindus in the parts where the outbreaks have been most frequent, stand in such fear of the Mapilla as mostly not to dare to press for their rights against them, and there is many a Mapilla tenant who does not pay his rent, and cannot, so imminent are the risks, be evicted".*

While there are several such testaments and reports that prove that the Malabar Genocide of Hindus was hardly a peasant uprising against the landlords, the narrative of the Left has prevailed over the years, whitewashing a heinous part of Hindu history.

Apart from direct testimonies that refute the 'peasant uprising' theory, there are at least 50 documented cases of Mapilla 'outrages' against Hindus in the same general area that give credence to the fact that the 1921 Genocide was not an isolated event where Muslims went on the war-path to murder Kafirs. .................. And here are those cases

> *It is not necessary to read each case in particular starting from number one to fifty; rather this "chronological record" is presented here for reference and evidence)*

One of the first recorded outbreaks, when Mapilla Muslims massacred Hindus due to fanaticism, is from 1836 and the process of mindless murder, loot and rape, intermittently continued till 1919. The Malabar genocide broke out in 1921 and the Khilafat movement was officially launched in 1920.

Here is a list of 50 such incidents as recorded by Diwan Bahadur C. Gopalan Nair, the then Deputy Collector of Calicut in his book:

1. 26th November 1836: In Pandalur Ernad, one Kallingal Kunholan stabbed one Chakku Pannikar who subsequently died of his wounds. He also wounded three others and was finally shot down by the Tahsildar on the 28th of November.

2. 15th April 1837: In Kalpatta, Ernad, one Ali Kutti of Chengara Amsom attacked and severely injured one Narayana Moosad and occupied his shop. The Tahsildar and Taluk peons then tried to control him, with the police shooting him down the next day.

3. 5th April 1839: In Pallipuram, Walluvanad one Thorayam Pulakal Athan and some other skilled one Kellil Raman and then set fire to a Hindu temple. They then hid in another Hindu temple where they were shot by the Taluk peon.

*And continued to*

47. 1896: In the book, Nair writes that for this particular atrocity that was unleashed on the Hindus, one was pressed to find any trigger. It was just a result of the unbridled Mohammadan fanaticism. On the 25th of February 1896, a gang of 20 Mapilla Muslims went on a killing spree from Chembrasseri Amsom and for 5 days, they terrorized the villages. The book says that during this period, Hindus were murdered and/or their Kudumis were cut off. They were forcefully converted to Islam as well. Temples were desecrated rampantly during this massacre and burnt down to ashes. On 1st March, the Muslims entered the Karanammulpad Temple, determined to make their last stand. Shots were exchanged with about 20 soldiers. At 9 AM, the District Magistrate with the main body of the troops and occupied the hill overlooking the temple at a distance of about 750 yards. When the police opened fire, instead of hiding, the Muslim fanatics purposely courted death while they were howling, shouting religious slogans and firing. Advancing steadily with frequent volleys over the broken ground, the police came near the temple to ask the Mapilla Muslims to surrender. The Muslims were defiant and the troops ended up entering the

temple without resistance. They ended up walking in on the dead bodies, with their throats slit of 92 Mapilla Muslims who had been murdered by Muslims themselves to ensure they were not captured alive.

48. April 1898: The Mapilla was 'revolting' in Payyanad. But the fanatics surrendered eventually.

49. 1915: In the year 1915, an attempt was made on the life of Mr. Innes, the District Magistrate. The Mapilla Muslims had then gone on a rampage, murdered and committing arson. They were finally shot down.

50. February 1919: A gang of fanatics headed by dismissed Mapilla head constable began to brew trouble. Following their usual methods they broke into and defiled several temples, killed almost every Brahmin and Nair who they came across and finally died at the hands of the police. 4 Brahmins and 2 Nairs had died in this incident.

After the 1919 incident, the Malabar Hindu Genocide broke out in August 1921 where over 10,000 Hindus were mercilessly killed. It was during these mindless fanatic killings by Mapilla Muslims that TL Strange was sent as a special commissioner to inquire why the Muslims were intermittently killing the Hindus. In his report, as mentioned above, he had categorically stated that the reason was mindless fanaticism of the Muslims and not a peasant revolt.

The three judges who had presided over a Special Tribunal in Calicut after the Malabar Genocide of Hindus had said:

*For the last hundreds of years at least, the Mapilla community has been disgraced from time to time by murderous outrages, as appears from the district Gazetteer. In the past, they have been due to fanaticism. They generally blazed out in the Ernad, Taluk, where the Moplahs were for the most part proselytes drawn from the dredges of the Hindu population. These men were miserably and hopelessly ignorant, and their untutored minds were particularly susceptible to the inflammatory teaching that Paradise was to be gained by killing Kaffirs, and the servants of Kaffirs. They would go out on the war path, killing Hindus, no matter whom, and would be joined by other fanatics and then seek death in hand-in-hand conflict with the troops. In some cases, they may have been inspired by hatred of a particular landlord, but no grievance seems to have been really necessary to start them on their wild careers. The Moplahs has been described as a barbarous and a savage race and unhappily the description seems appropriate at the present day. But it was not mere fanaticism, it was not agrarian trouble, it was not* destitution that *worked on the minds of Ali Musalair and his followers. The evidence conclusively shows that it was the influence of the Khilafat and the non-cooperation movements that drove them to their crime. It is this which distinguishes the present from all previous outbreaks. Their intention was, absurd though it may seem, to subvert the British Government and to substitute a Khilafat Government by force of arms.*

This was an excerpt from the Judgment in case number 7 of 1921 on the file of Special Tribunal, Calicut.This judgment itself clearly shows that for 100 years before 1921, Mapilla Muslims had gone on the warpath and massacred Hindus. They did so then owing to their Islamic fanaticism. What was different about the 1921 genocide of Hindus was not that they were doing it to support India's freedom struggle but to establish a Khilafat Government enlace of the British. A Khilafat government here means nothing but an Islamic caliphate. It is to be kept in mind that this was the movement summarily and wholeheartedly supported by Mohandas Karamchand Gandhi. To date, the narrative about the Malabar Hindu Genocide has been distorted to whitewash the horrors faced by the Hindus of Malabar, to insinuate that the murders of Hindus were retribution for Hindu landlords mistreating Muslim peasants. The reality, however, is far from it. *The above mentioned documented jihad is enough to prove the character of Mopilla – and no one will dare to expect good ............. from them but Mr. Gandhi believed them and supported "**Khilafat movement**"*

### End of Chaptor I

# Mapilla

# Riot

# Hindu

# Genocide

# Chapter II

## Mapilla Genocide

_Had there been no Gandhi and congress should have not supported Khilafat andolan, the movement might have not gone wrong and tens of thousands of lives of innocent Hindu would have been saved. Womanhood would have been saved and also large amount of property including houses of Hindu would have been saved if Mr. Gandhi would have not been there._

# Chapter II

## Mapilla Hindu Genocide, 1921:

The Mapilla Hindu Genocide, or the Malabar Rebellion, or the Mappila Rebellion, or the Mapilla Riots refer to a series of incidents in the history of mankind, where Hindus were not only butchered, but the entire incident was either wiped out from history in entirety, or was twisted to fit into a pre-decided story. *The Mapilla Rebellion of 1921-22 was a rebellion gone wrong*, where the rebels targeted Hindus, apart from attacking the British Raj.

It is important to know who were Mapilla, how and why the Malabar Rebellion started, and why it went wrong.

## WHO WERE MAPPILAS?

The term "Mapilla" is from Malayalam and translates to "honored/great child," referring to all the "guests" or invaders to Kerala, especially in the Malabar region. Mapilla were some of the earliest Muslims settled in South Asia, and had a direct connection with Arab, through spice trade routes with the Gulf. Till 1498, the Mappilas lived & grew their trades in the region, due to the tolerance shown by Hindus. During this period, inter-faith marriages between Hindus & Muslims were common, and many Hindus converted to Islam due to marriages (whereas there is no account of Mappilas converting to Hinduism).

On the arrival of Europeans like Vasco da Gama in 1498, Mappilas were sidelined, their trade & commerce squeezed, and Arab trade routes curtailed. Mappilas were not entitled to inherit any lands, which were owned by Hindus. Mappilas were shown no tolerance by European imperialists, who persecuted them commercially and otherwise, leading to a growing animosity in the Mappilas towards

Hindus, who they started to see as their rivals, as well as towards Europeans.

"The Portuguese attitude reflected the medieval European tradition, and was well represented by the governor of Goa, Afonso Albuquerque (d 1515), who dreamt of destroying Mecca and who bitterly persecuted his Mappila opponents."

*The Supreme Muslim Council: Islam under the British Mandate for Palestine, p 459,*

This brand of "pepper politics" shown by Portuguese, then Dutch (1656), then British (1662), then French (1775), led to militancy and religious fanaticism in Mapillas, who were now landless & poor & persecuted by Christian lords. During the reign of Hyder Ali (1782) and Tipu Sultan (1799), the Mapilla gained some prominence, but the hatred towards Hindus, sown by Islamic invaders, took permanent ground. When the British gained full power (1792), the hopes of the Mappilas to prosper were squashed, and they were bitterer than ever before.

## KHILAFAT MOVEMENT, NON-COOPERATION MOVEMENT INSTIGATED THE MOPLAH REBELLION

The Khilafat movement was an uprising of Indian Muslims in support of the Islamic caliphate, in the wake of World War I. It was aimed at Islamic dominion over India, by destroying the British Empire, with support from the Ottoman Empire (which was eventually exterminated in late 1922).

The Khilafat Movement, led by the Ali brothers, had full support of M. K. Gandhi, who promised the support of Hindus as well, to the Ali brothers—Shaukat Ali, Mohammad Ali Jauhar and Abul Kalam Azad—knowing full well that they would attack Hindus should they fail to support them. _The Ali brothers had clearly informed M. K. Gandhi that if the Afghans invaded India to wage "holy war" or Jihad, they would fight not just the British, but the Hindus as well_. Gandhi agreed to this, and asked Hindus to support the Khilafat

Movement, and to submit to the dictates of the Mohammedans in matters of controversy.

"The Imperial Government have knowingly flouted religious sentiments dearly cherished by the 70 millions Mussalmans...If the Mussalmans of India offer non-cooperation to Government in order to secure justice on the Khilafat, it is the duty of every Hindu to cooperate with their Moslem brethren."

*M. K. Gandhi's speech to 20,000 people. Mapilla Rebellion 1921, C. Gopalan Nair, p 19-22*

Khilafat Movement gained force in Malabar as well, due to his patronage, and fueled the Malabar or Mapilla Rebellion.

"Last month Gandhi wrote in Young India: *"For him he can clearly see the time coming when he must refuse obedience to every single State-made law, even though there may be a certainty of bloodshed."* The Ali brothers, who were kept under restraint during the Great War and the Afghan War, for being in traitorous correspondence with our foreign enemies—a crime for which they should have been tried and punished—have been set free, and openly state that they would do all they can to help the Afghans in the event of a Jihad against the British in India, calling upon all true Mohammadans to do likewise. They have been allowed to preach that doctrine in Malabar in spite of the protest of the District Magistrate, who was not allowed to prohibit the seditious meetings. Can there be any reasonable doubt that this was the main cause of the Mapilla rebellion?"

*Extract of letter by Sir Michael O' Dwyer to Daily Telegraph.*

The Congress, under the leadership of M. K. Gandhi, supported the Khilafat Movement, under the garb of the non-cooperation movement, which spread to Malabar.

"The Congress had adopted the principle of non-co-operation; Khilafat and non-co-operation movements were indistinguishable; Every Mapilla centre had a Khilafat association, with a Mapilla president, a Mapilla secretary and a majority of Mapilla members."

*Mapilla Rebellion 1921, C. Gopalan Nair, p 19*

The Mapilla rebels were armed with knives and ammunition, and had *planned the attack* on the British, and Hindus, lest they fail them. They asked the Hindu landowners to give them weapons, and the trusting Hindus, not knowing what was headed their way, gave them knives which would eventually slit their own throats.

## MAPPILLA REBELLION
## AN OUTCOME OF JIHAD

Many scholars have argued that the Mappila rebellions (and earlier outbreaks) were an outcome of agrarian troubles and economic distress. But this was not the case. If that were so, Hindus who were working as peasants had the same opportunity and motive to rebel against the *jenmis*, or against the earlier Islamic rulers while they were in power and oppressed Hindus. But instead, Hindus of Malabar had fled and abandoned their homes during the reign of Hyder Ali & Tipu Sultan.

"Agrarian grievances were obviously not sufficient to spark violence in the rural

Malabar among the Mappillas, or the agricultural population in general. It is the Islamic character of the Mapilla outbreaks that suggests why they cannot be tied to the eviction rate, and why none occurred among the Hindu population. All of the outbreaks, even those that had agrarian grievances as the immediate cause, were conducted in an unmistakable Islamic idiom – the Jihad. Each was expressed as a religious act because the Mapilla were inspired by the militant teachings of a small group of Mappilla religious leaders."

*Dale, S. (1975). The Mapilla Outbreaks: Ideology and Social Conflict in Nineteenth-Century Kerala. The Journal of Asian Studies, 35(1), 85-97.*

**The Mappilla rebellion was a bigger catastrophe for Hindus than the earlier outbreaks, because it was an organized movement, amplified by the Khilafat movement, which made it a planned crime, rather than discrete outbreaks by discontent religious militants.**

"...in 1921, the Khilafat movement added the crucial elements of ideology and organization to the pre-existing traditions of religious militancy and social conflict. It was this addition, more than anything else that distinguished the Mappilla rebellion from all the earlier outbreaks."

*Dale, S. (1975). The Mappilla Outbreaks: Ideology and Social Conflict in Nineteenth-Century Kerala. The Journal of Asian Studies, 35(1), 85-97.*

## THE MOPLAH REBELLION GONE WRONG

The few Hindus of Malabar who had joined the non-cooperation movement were not prepared for the violence & wreckage the Mohammedans had planned.

"Distressed by the violence, most Malabar Hindus withdrew from the struggle, which, by default, became the Mapilla revolt."

*The Supreme Muslim Council: Islam under the British Mandate for Palestine by Uri M. Kupferschmidt, p 459*

Hindus withdrew from the Malabar rebellion almost as soon as it broke out. **This incurred** the wrath of the *Jihadi* Mapillas on the Hindus apart from the British, who were trying to contain the troops of rebels.

The rebellion continued for 6 months, during which period, atrocities of every kind were meted out to Hindus. It had severe fallout for the Mapillas as well. More than 200 Mapillas were executed, 502 were sentenced to life imprisonment, and approximately 50,000 were imprisoned or exiled to Andaman, and heavy fines were levied on them by the British government. The zealotry exhibited by the Mapillas was shocking, and it was evident that their war was not just for liberation from British, but for Islamic dominance.

## ATROCITIES ON HINDUS IN THE MAPILLA REBELLION

During the entire Mapilla Rebellion, unspeakable, unimaginable atrocities were committed against Hindus, which is why it should rightly be called the *Mapilla Hindu Genocide.* By not doing so, a severe injustice will be done to those who gave their lives and livelihoods due to the Islamic Jihad waged on them.

The total figure of **at least 2,500 Hindus brutally slaughtered**, and another 2500 forcibly converted, is quoted in several accounts. Other brutalities include violating the modesty of women, butchering children, and forcing Hindus into submission and death. These atrocities were reported in international news dailies and accounts of the district magistrates and other police officials.

"In the Arya Samaj registers alone 1766 cases of forced converts have been recorded and if the figures from all relief committees were collected, their number is sure to exceed 2500."

*Pundit Rishi Ram's Letter, Moplah Rebellion 1921, C. Gopalan Nair , p 119*

It was confirmed on an international level that the Moplah Rebellion was, indeed, a "holy war" or Jihad, in accordance with the Khilafat movement.

THE MALABAR REBELLION.

PRIMARILY A HOLY WAR.

ALLAHABAD, Sunday Morning.—
The Malabar rebellion is primarily a
holy war. Green flags have been
planted and there is a forcible conversion of Hindus. Wholesale arson and
looting is continuing and more murders have been committed. The non-
co-operation fanatics are proclaiming a
complete swaraj and a famine is threatened consequent on the great destruction of the lines. These, however,
have been restored, except ten miles,
which was much damaged. A strong
force is advancing for the relief of
Malapuram, and the situation is becoming gradually localised.

"The Malabar Rebellion. Primarily a Holy War.

Allahabad, Sunday Morning— The Malabar rebellion is primarily a holy war. Green flags have been planted and there is forcible conversion of Hindus. Wholesale arson and looting is continuing and more murders have been committed. The non co-operation fanatics are proclaiming a complete swaraj and a famine is threatened consequent on the great destruction of the lines..."

*Daily Telegraph (Launceston, Tas. : 1883 – 1928), Monday 29 Aug, 1921. Retrieved via http://bit.ly/2XEMwwa*

Hindus were exterminated systematically, to the shock of the British officers as well. They did not anticipate such mass violence against Hindus by the Moplahs.

"Malabar Rebellion

Moplah Atrocities

Allahabad, Wednesday. At Kuttipuram, 200 Moplahs, with swords and knives, raided the police station and wounded five constables. Diabolical atrocities are reported. Hindus being forced to dig their own graves before they are butchered. One was flayed alive for helping the troops, and two policemen were hacked to death near Nilambur.

Refugees are pouring into the troop centers, but there are difficulties in provisioning even for the military. They report that the extermination of Hindus is proceeding systematically but favored women and girls are retained."

*World (Hobart, Tas.: 1918 – 1924), Friday, 7 Oct, 1921. Retrieved via http://bit.ly/2XE4cbd*

Moplahs committed every type of atrocity on Hindus, from slaughtering their cattle, to murder, arson, loot, and sexually assaulting women.

"Moplah Rebellion. Reckless Butchery.

Hindus Refusing Islam. Allahabad, Thursday

"....The rebels are conducting a reckless butchery of all Hindus refusing Islam. Some districts are empty of Hindus..."

*Advocate (Burnie, Tas. : 1890 – 1954), 8 October, 1921. Retrieved via http://bit.ly/2XBDq3x*

The situation for Hindus kept getting worse, as the days progressed.

"Malabar Rebellion

Slaughtering Hindus | Unrest at Madras

Allahabad, Friday—Calicut is overflowing with refugees reporting that the Moplahs are now not offering the choice of conversion, but are slaughtering Hindus indiscriminately. Reinforcement for the British troop guard is arriving..."

*World (Hobart, Tas.: 1918 – 1924), Monday, 10 Oct, 1921. Retrieved via http://bit.ly/2XEMCnw*

The Moplah rebellion turned most of the Hindus in that region into refugees. As the rebellion progressed, more and more Hindus were internally displaced, and took refuge in the refugee camps or in the jungles.

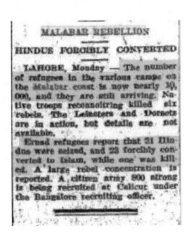

Malabar Rebellion | Hindus Forcibly Converted

Lahore, Monday— the number of refugees in the various camps on the Malabar Coast is now nearly 10,000 and they are still arriving. Native troops reconnoitering killed six rebels...Ernad refugees report that 31 Hindus were seized, and 23 forcibly converted to Islam, while one was killed..."

*World (Hobart, Tas.: 1918 – 1924), Wednesday, 9 Nov, 1921. Retrieved via http://bit.ly/2XD3tHt*

The total number of Hindu refugees is estimated at **more than 26,000.** Accounts of Arya Samaj, which arrived in Kerala to provide relief to Hindus, reports a number of 26,000 in their relief camps alone.

"From October, Concentration Camps were formed with kitchen relief in Calicut and rice doles in the mofussil. As the numbers of refugees increased, day by day, new camps were opened. Within a few weeks there were 22 camps in all with about 26,000 refugees of all castes and creeds."

*Moplah Rebellion 1921, C. Gopalan Nair, p 96*

But the Moplah atrocities were not limited to butchering Hindus. Moplahs made it their mission to defile and destroy every Hindu temple in the Malabar region.

"No statistics have been compiled, but the number of temples destroyed or desecrated must exceed 100. The number is probably large, but for obvious reasons the Government have purposely refrained from attempting to collect accurate figures."

*Legislative Council interpellation, November 14th '22, quoted in 'Moplah Rebellion 1921,' C. Gopalan Nair, p 88*

No village was spared, and all temples in the area were either razed to the ground or defiled.

"There is hardly a village that has not its own temple, in the majority of villages there is more than one, and almost every temple in the rebel area has been desecrated."

*Moplah Rebellion 1921, C. Gopalan Nair, p 89*

**The women of Malabar wrote to the Countess of Reading, apprising her of the**

**ruthless butchery of Hindus and religious defilement of Hindu temples and places of worship.**

"Your Ladyship is not fully apprised of all the horrors and atrocities perpetrated by the fiendish rebels: of the many wells and tanks filled up with the mutilated but often only half dead bodies of our nearest and dearest ones who refused to abandon the faith of our Fathers; of pregnant women cut to pieces and left on the roadside and in the jungles, with the unborn babe protruding from the mangled corpse; of our innocent and helpless children torn from our arms and done to death before our eyes and our husbands and fathers tortured, flayed and burnt alive; ...of thousands of our homesteads reduced to cindermounds out of sheer savagery and wanton spirit of destruction; of our places of worship desecrated and destroyed and of the images of the deity shamefully insulted by putting the entrails of slaughtered cows where flower garlands used to lie, or else smashed to pieces; of the wholesale looting of hard earned wealth of generations, reducing many who were formerly rich and prosperous to publicly beg for a piece or two in the streets of Calicut..."

*Memorial submitted by Hindu women of Malabar to Countess of Reiding, quoted in Moplah Rebellion 1921, C. Gopalan Nair*

There is no shortage of accounts of Hindu refugees reporting their plight, of lives destroyed, of kins lost, of religion defiled. It is incontrovertible that the Malabar Rebellion of Moplahs, was, indeed, the biggest assault on Hindus in the history of British India yet.

The volunteers of Arya Samaj performed the sincere task of reconverting those Hindus who were forcibly converted by Moplahs. A simple *"prayaschitta"* was given to them by the priests of Arya Samaj, upon which they were once again accepted back as Hindus. But the wounds of the deadly Hindu Genocide take longer to heal, and leave scars. The demography and turmoil's faced by Kerala, along with the irreligious sentiment of many Hindus of Kerala, is, in some ways, related to the gory history of Malabar and attacks on Hindus.

## Khilafat Movement

Diwan Bahadur C. Gopalan Nair in his book, 'The Moplah Rebellion 1921', writes thus:

*...it was not mere fanaticism, it was not agrarian trouble, and it was not destitution that worked on the minds of Ali Musaliar and his followers. The evidence conclusively shows that it was the influence of the Khilafat and Non-co-operation movements that drove them to their crime.* It is this which distinguishes the present from all previous outbreaks. Their intention was, absurd though it may seem, to subvert the British Government and to substitute a Khilafat Government by force of arms. (Judgment in Case No. 7 of 1921 on the file of the Special Tribunal, Calicut.) ...

Nair noted Ali Musliyar rose to prominence at the instance of a Khilafat conference held in Karachi. Furthermore, Musliyar was not a native of Tirurangadi. He had only moved in 14 years earlier. So, according to Nair, there was not class revolt he was handling. It was a Khilafat edifice prepared and passed from distant Karachi, possibly controlled by spiritual leaders of Islam.

1. The Khilafat movement was introduced into the district of Malabar on 28 April 1920, by a Resolution at the Malabar District Conference, held at Manjeri, the headquarters of Ernad Taluk.

2. On 30 March 1921, there was a meeting at which one Abdulla Kutti Musaliar of Vayakkad lectured on Khilafat, in Kizhakoth Amsom, Calicut Taluk.

3. And at a second meeting held the next day at Pannur Mosque,

4. There was some unpleasantness between the Mappilas on one side, and Nairs and Tiyyar, who resented the Khilafat meeting, on the other.

5. The Mapillas mustered the strength to attack the place of worship belonging to the Hindu Adhigari of the village.

## Nature of attacks

The Malabar Rebellion witnessed many attacks on British officers in the region. The Madras High Court, which adjudicated in this matter, had passed judgments on each of the cases against the various Mapilla rioters who were captured. The Madras High Court said on the matter,

It appears also that on the night of the 20th of August, at Nilambur 16 miles from Manjeri a police constable at Edavanna, were murdered and at Tiruvangadi in addition to Mr. Rowley and Lieutenant Johnston nine other persons were murdered. The police station at Manjeri was attacked on the night of the 21st; public officers at Manjeri on the 22nd. On the 24th of August Variyamkunnath Kunhahammad Haji who is described as the rebel leader arrived at Manjeri. All these incidents had occurred when the respondent made the speech already referred to, and it was in such dangerous surroundings that he made it and the reference to Tiruvangadi in that speech has a consequence, a particular significance. Subsequent events are that on the 26th of August a retired police inspector was murdered at Anakayam near Manjeri by Variyamkunnath Kunhahammad Haji and his followers and on the 25th of August his head was paraded on a spear; and it was common ground that the respondent was at Manjeri from the morning of the 21st of August until the 30th of August.

The District Magistrate stated that reliable information had been received about 180 forced conversions of Hindus and the actual total may run into thousands. Roland E. Miller estimates forced conversions as in the range of 200 and 2500. In the aftermath of this ethnic cleansing, the Suddhi Movement was created by the Arya Samaj. They converted over 2,000 Hindus who had been forcibly converted to Islam by the Mappilas. Sumit Sarkar in Modern India quotes an Arya Samaj source that claimed about 600 Hindus were killed and 2,500 forcibly converted during the rebellion. Variamkunnath Kunjahammad Hajji claimed to have killed the alleged British agents and spies responsible for the forced conversion of Hindus to Muslim and killing others. However, their leader, Swami Shraddhananda was stabbed on 23 December 1926 by an Islamist at his Ashram.

## Important Quotes

**B. R. Ambedkar** said on the rebellion:

The blood-curdling atrocities committed by the Mapilla in Malabar against the Hindus were indescribable. All over Southern India, a wave of horrified feeling had spread among the Hindus of every shade of opinion, which was intensified when certain Khilafat leaders were so misguided as to pass resolutions of congratulations to the Mapilla on the brave fight they were conducting for the sake of religion". Any person could have said that this was too heavy a price for Hindu-Muslim unity. But Mr. Gandhi was so much obsessed by the necessity of establishing Hindu-Muslim unity that he was prepared to make light of the doings of the Mapilla and the Khilafats who were congratulating them. He spoke of the Mapilla the "brave God-fearing Mapilla who were fighting for what they consider as religion and in a manner which they consider as religious ".

**_B. R. Ambedkar_** said on the rebellion:

The Hindus were visited by a dire fate at the hands of the Mapilla. Massacres, forcible conversions, desecration of temples, foul outrages upon women, such as ripping open pregnant women, pillage, arson and destruction— in short, all the accompaniments of brutal and unrestrained barbarism, were perpetrated freely by the Mapillas upon the Hindus until such time as troops could be hurried to the task of restoring order through a difficult and extensive tract of the country.

This was not a Hindu-Moslem riot. This was just a Bartholomew. The number of Hindus, who were killed, wounded or converted, is not known. But the number must have been enormous.

**_Annie Besant,_** who wanted dominion status for India, opposed non-cooperation movement, supported Montague-Chelmsford reforms, who had adverse effect on her popularity due to difference of opinion and later left the political field, recounts in two separate articles in New India on 29 November 1921 and 6 December 1921 as to what happened to the Malabar Hindus at the hands of the Moplahs:

Mr. Gandhi...can he not feel a little sympathy for thousands of women left with only rags, driven from home, for little children born of the flying mothers on roads in refugee camps? The misery is beyond description. Girl wives, pretty and sweet, with eyes half blind with weeping, distraught with terror; women who have seen their husbands hacked to pieces before their eye, in the way "Mapilla consider as religious"; old women tottering, whose faces become written with anguish and who cry at a gentle touch...men who have lost all, hopeless, crushed, desperate...Can you conceive of a more ghastly and inhuman crime than the murders of babies and pregnant women?...A pregnant woman carrying 7 months was cut through the abdomen by a rebel and she was seen lying dead on the way with the dead child projecting out of the womb...Another: a baby of six months was snatched away from the breast of his own mother and cut into two pieces... Are these rebels' human beings or monsters?

A respectable <u>Nayar</u> Lady at Melatur was stripped naked by the rebels in the presence of her husband and brothers, who were made to stand close by with their hands tied behind. When they shut their eyes in abhorrence they were compelled at the point of sword to open their eyes and witness the rape committed by the brute in their presence.

### *Annie Besant said on the rebellion:*

"They established the Khilafat Raj, crowned a King, murdered and plundered abundantly, and killed or drove away all Hindus who would not apostatize. Somewhere about a lakh people were driven from their homes with nothing but the clothes they had on, stripped of everything."

Here is the text of Resolution No. 3 of the Ahmedabad session of the INC, where Gandhiji was appointed as its sole executive authority, on 24 December 1921, in connection with the Moplah Riots:

**The Rani of Nilambur**

in a petition to Lady Reading:

But it is possible that your Ladyship is not fully apprised of all the horrors and atrocities perpetrated by the fiendish rebels; of the many wells and tanks filled up with the mutilated, but often only half dead bodies of our nearest and dearest ones who refused to abandon the faith of our fathers; of pregnant women cut to pieces and left on the roadsides and in the jungles, with the unborn babe protruding from the mangled corpse; of our innocent and helpless children torn from our arms and done to death before our eyes and of our husbands and fathers tortured, flayed and burnt alive; of our hapless sisters forcibly carried away from the midst of kith and kin and subjected to every shame and outrage which the vile and brutal imagination of these inhuman hell-hounds could conceive of; of thousands of our homesteads reduced to cinder-mounds out of sheer savagery and a wanton spirit of destruction; of our places of worship desecrated and destroyed and of the images of the deity shamefully insulted by putting the entrails of slaughtered cows where flower garlands used to lie or else smashed to pieces; of the wholesale looting of hard-earned wealth of generations reducing many who were formerly rich and prosperous to publicly beg for a piece or two in the streets of Calicut, to buy salt or chilly or betel-leaf - rice being mercifully provided by the various relief agencies.

## Conclusion

**_B. R. Ambedkar_** said on the rebellion:

The Hindus were visited by a dire fate at the hands of the Moplas. Massacres, forcible conversions, desecration of temples, foul outrages upon women, such as ripping open pregnant women, pillage, arson and destruction— in short, all the accompaniments of brutal and unrestrained barbarism, were perpetrated freely by the Moplas upon the Hindus until such time as troops could be hurried to the task of restoring order through a difficult and extensive tract of the country. This was not a Hindu-Moslem riot. This was just a Bartholomew. The number of Hindus who were killed, wounded or converted is not known. But the number must have been enormous.

**_Annie Besant,_** who wanted dominion status for India, opposed <u>non-cooperation movement</u>, supported <u>Montague-Chelmsford reforms</u>, who had adverse effect on her popularity due to difference of opinion and later left the political field, recounts in two separate articles in New India on 29 November 1921 and 6 December 1921 as to what happened to the Malabar Hindus at the hands of the Moplahs:

**_B. R. Ambedkar_** said on the rebellion:

The blood-curdling atrocities committed by the Moplas in Malabar against the Hindus were indescribable. All over Southern India, a wave of horrified feeling had spread among the Hindus of every shade of opinion, which was intensified when certain Khilafat leaders were so misguided as to pass resolutions of congratulations to the Moplas on the brave fight they were conducting for the sake of religion". Any person could have said that this was too heavy a price for Hindu-Muslim unity.

But Mr. Gandhi was so much obsessed by the necessity of establishing Hindu-Muslim unity that he was prepared to make light of the doings of the Moplas and the Khilafats who were congratulating them. He spoke of the Mapillas as the *"brave God-fearing Moplahs who were fighting for what they consider as religion and in a manner which they consider as religious ".*

*This is what Malabar, in particular, owes to the Khilafat agitation, to Gandhi and his Hindu friends."*

Chapter III

# The
# Kohat
# Genocide

*an effect continued from*
*Mopilla Genocide 1921*

facebook.com/Old Pictures Of Kohat
2nd day of Hindu-Muslim Riots in Kohat.    September, 1924

The Khilafat movement or the Caliphate movement was of the Indian Muslims against the British colonial rule in India. The movement started by Indian Muslim leaders also sought to restore the caliph of the Ottoman Caliphate in Turkey. In a highly contentious decision, Mahatma Gandhi had announced his support for the Khilafat movement, who himself was leading the non-cooperation at that time. Gandhi had dreamt of achieving Indian independence through 'Hindu-Muslim unity', and thus compelled the Congress party to hands with the Muslim

League against British India. However, the Khilafat movement had died by 1922 due to a change of policy in Turkey.

After the Khilafat movement began to fade, communal tension brewing underneath the facade of 'Hindu-Muslim unity' surfaced. On the fateful days of September 9th and 10th of 1924, radical Islamist mobs unleashed mayhem in Hindu *mohallas* (neighborhood) in Kohat town of North-West Frontier Province (now known as Khyber Pakhtunkhwa) in present-day Pakistan. The carnage was pre-meditated venture and resulted in the ***exodus of the entire Hindu population from the area.***

Kohat had a Muslim population of 12000 while the number of Hindus and Sikhs stood at a mere 5000 (Census 1921). The Hindus were prosperous even though they were outnumbered. The Hindu community lived in urban areas and controlled large businesses.

Despite this, a large number of Hindus were being converted to Islam (about 150 conversions each year between 1919 and 1924). The Hindus had the support of the Arya Samaj and the Sanatan Dharma Sabha..

There was widespread resentment amongst the Muslims for the minority Hindus and the Kohat riots were a manifestation of long-standing friction. ***A fertile ground, conducive to riots, was being created by giving a communal twist to each incident***. When the son of one Sardar Makan Singh eloped with a Muslim girl, it motivated the Islamic clerics to give inflammatory speeches and provoke the community. Another dispute over a bathing tank was alleviated as a 'Hindu-Muslim' issue.

One of the key factors that added fuel to the fire of communalism was the publication of a highly objectionable and 'blasphemous' poem in May 1924 by a notorious Muslim-centric newspaper named *Lahaul*. It read,

**"We shall have to burn the Gita of Kirars.
We shall break the flute of Krishna.**

**O Muslims!**
**You will have to take up the sword**
**and destroy the existence of Kirars**
**and burn their goddesses. "**

The genocidal poem by a Muslim newspaper hurt the sentiments of the Hindu community and especially the Sanatan Dharma Sabha. The local secretary of the organization, Jiwan Das, then published a pamphlet by the name of 'Krishan Sandesh'. The pamphlet contained poems meant to reinstate the religious identity among the Hindus. Miffed by the anti-Hindu poem published in Lahaul, Das printed a poem by one author from Jammu wherein he mocked the followers of Allah. It read,

"**We have kept quiet so long;**
**we shall have to speak out,**
**O mullah!**
**You must gather up your prayer carpet**
**and taken it to Arabia.**
**We shall build a temple to Vishnu in place**
**of the Ka'ba,**
**And destroy the existence of the Nimaziz. "**

Das printed 1000 copies of the contentious poem in retaliation to the *Lahaul* poem and distributed the pamphlets at the Janam Ashtami festival.

This infuriated the Muslim community while their press and ulemas added fuel to the fire. Inflammatory speeches were made by Muslim leaders in mosques in Kohat. On September 3, 1924, Maulvi Ahmed Gul and Qazi Miraj Din led a Muslim crowd to the Assistant Commissioner of Police, S. Ahmad Khan, and demanded action against Jiwan Das. Khan assured them that Jiwan Das would be prosecuted under IPC 505, 153A. He had also directed the burning of pamphlets.

The Hindu community had meanwhile 'conceded' that the pamphlets were offensive and passed on the blame to Sanatan Dharma Sabha. They had asked for a pardon but opposed the burning of pamphlets since they contained the portrait of Lord Krishna on the covers. On September 8, Jiwan Das was released on bail and asked to leave the district until the conclusion of the trial. Ulemas used mosques for provocation, Islamists took 'oath of talaq'

*"Alas!*
*Oh impotent Mussulmans!*
*You have spoiled your cause by accepting*
*bribes from the Hindus.*
*You should die!*
*You should have some sense of shame,"*

the extremist preaching's begun at the mosque. Maulvi Ahmed Gul then set the stage for the impending riots. He warned the police to take action against Das or that the community would take action as per *Shariat*. He gave an ultimatum until 8 am on September 9. He received support from other clerics such as Shahin Shah and Mian Fazul Shah.

In one such meeting at Haji Bahadur mosque, fanatic Muslims took the 'oath of talaq' i.e. they will divorce their wives if they fail to defend their religion. By night, Muslims were seen parading with arms. On September 9, 1924, a crowd of 1000-1500 Muslims first went to meet Deputy Commissioner Reilly, forcing him to give in to their demands. At around mid-day, half of the mob disappeared and surfaced outside the Hindu mohalla. The Hindus were anticipating trouble after learning about the 'oath of talaq', and hate speeches delivered at mosques. They sent telegrams to the Deputy Commissioner, SP but in vain.

### Kohat riots: Remembering the carnage of September 9-10

Muslim mobs, particularly young boys, stormed into Hindu colonies and began wielding sticks and pelting stones. The house of one Sardar Makan Singh was burnt and his garden was destroyed. Fearing an impending program, the Hindus fired shots at them. _Amidst the chaos, one of the stone palters died while several others were injured_. **This gave the fanatic Muslim mob a free pass to kill the Hindus.** Shops, temples and houses were set on fire and destroyed. Properties belonging to the Hindus were vandalized and looted.

The riots continued until 7 pm in the night when the law enforcement authorities dispersed the frenzied mob and brought the situation under control. However, the police did not prepare for another round of violence and killings that was to occur the following day. At about 11 am on September 10, 4000 Muslims from Kohat and nearby tribal areas gathered outside the Hindu mohalla and resumed one of the deadliest episodes of violence in pre-Independent India. The large-scale arson forced about 3000 Hindus to flee the Kohat town and take shelter in a nearby temple. It was at this point that the Muslims began torching Hindu homes after looting them and slaughtering those who chose to stay behind.

Reportedly, the fire took over a week to extinguish and almost the entire Hindu mohalla was burnt to ashes. The Hindus of Kohat sought refuge in Rawalpindi in Punjab. It was estimated that the casualties on the Hindu side were 3 times more than that of Muslims, some of whom were killed in self-defense. Official statistics state that 12 Hindus were killed, 13 went missing (presumably killed), and 86 were wounded. The total casualties stood at 155. *The entire Hindu population of Kohat was wiped out, forcing a further demographic change in favor of the Muslims.*

The fear and panic created by the riots prevented the return of Hindus, who were forced to leave their homes. The return of the exiled Hindus began from January 1925 onwards after NWFP Chief Commissioner H.N. Bolton facilitated a settlement between Hindu and Muslim leaders. As per the settlement which yet again favored the Muslims, all civil/criminal cases pertaining to the riots were dropped except for the charges of blasphemy against Jiwan Das. The Hindu victims of the riots did not get any compensation but were offered loans of 5 lakh rupees for damages.

### The Faith of the British Raj on 'Muslims'

Prior to the Kohat riots of 1924, Lord Reading wrote to the British Secretary of State on July 23 stating, "The Gandhi movement could never have gained its strength but for the Treaty of Sevres which made the Mohamedans so fanatic that they joined up with the Hindus for the time being...the difficulty at present is to keep the Mohamedan and Hindu from each other's throats, a task which I believe can only be performed by the British....From purely Indian considerations, I have no hesitation in saying that the peace [with Turkey] will assure us of the support of all but the extremists among the 60 or 70 million Mohamedans in India and will help materially to strengthen the British position in India."

## The influence of Ulemas, Khilafat movement and its aftermath

Patrick Mc Ginn wrote, "The heightened sense of religious identity which existed among the Muslim community was accentuated during the Khilafat movement. The orthodox ulama had been brought into political activity on a large scale. They had been a valuable asset in the Non-co-operation and Khilafat movements in gaining support among the masses. With the decline of these movements the ulama were no longer needed as politicians turned away from mass politics. As a result, their influence disappeared temporarily."

He added, "The activities of the ulama in the years following Khilafat can be seen as an effort to perpetuate power and influence within the Muslim community. *Communal issues became more important at the local level.* Those Muslim leaders who had been heavily involved in the Khilafat movement became the defenders of the faith in subsequent years." *While Gandhi piggybacked on the Khilafat movement to artificially forge a 'Hindu Muslim unity', the underlying religious antagonism did not remain concealed for long. To correct the discourse he fasted for 21 days to restore communal harmony.*

*A closer analysis of the Khilafat movement tells us that the seeds of prominent historical events such as the partition of India on religious grounds, the creation of Pakistan, and the genesis of Hindustan were either sowed or germinated in this movement.*

Be it the genocide of 10000 Hindus during the Moplah Massacre of 1921 or the exodus of the entire Hindu population in Kohat town of northwest Frontier Provinces in 1924, **the true face of 'Islamic fundamentalism' was exposed.**

Even post-partition, the seeds of *Islamic supremacy and fanaticism* culminated in the exodus of Kashmiri Pandits from the Muslim-dominated Kashmir valley. The plight of Hindus has remained unchanged since then and they have paid the price with their lives each time.

## End of Chapter III

## "DIRECT ACTION" DAY ASSAULTS

### WIDESPREAD LOOTING & INCENDIARISM

FROM OUR CALCUTTA OFFICE

AUGUST 16.—STABBING, ARSON, LOOTING AND WILFUL DESTRUCTION ON A LARGE SCALE WERE WIDESPREAD IN CALCUTTA TODAY, WHICH HAD BEEN DECLARED "DIRECT ACTION DAY" BY THE MUSLIM LEAGUE.

Over 170 persons were killed and over 1,000 injured during the day, about 75 per cent of the latter having been admitted into six of the main hospitals in the city.

CURFEW was declared from 9 p.m. to 4 a.m., but in spite of this incidents continued throughout the night. Mobile police patrols toured the city throughout the day, dispersing crowds bent on mischief. Police are reported to have fired on a number of occasions, and about a dozen deaths in the hospitals were due to bullet wounds.

The Calcutta Fire Brigade worked at full pressure and dealt with more than 200 fires, large and small, under police protection. Many fires, especially in the bustee areas, could not be tackled as crowds prevented the Fire Brigade men from reaching them.

Apart from the damage caused by arson, the financial loss incurred by shopkeepers and private individuals through looting alone may total scores of lakhs.

Public transport services, including taxis, gharries and rickshaws were at a complete standstill, vehicular traffic on the roads being confined mainly to ambulances, police patrol vans and a few private cars.

*Chapter IV*

# The
# Great
# Calcutta
# Killing

### The Direct Action Day
### of 16 AUG 1946

Quit India movement has been successfully suppressed by British Government as almost the entire congress leaders had been imprisoned. However effort of Subhash Chandra Bose was in progress but even this one was finally defeated. However the defeat of INA initiated a chain of reaction i.e. like a serial blast in the shape of mutiny and a country wide protest of the trial of INA officers and to support mutiny. Commensurate to this militant activism Mr. Atlee had a discussion with Churchill on19-02-46 in the House of Commons on the issue of holding in India and it must be expected that Mr. Jinna was been informed about it.

Crisp Mission was been sent in India to find out the way of a peaceful handover of power. These events might have given enough indication about liberation of the country in which Pakistan was an internal issue. Mr. Jinnah was not needed to take a Heroic pose and extraordinary enthusiasm to declare one

# "*Direct Action Day*".
## Islamic supremacy and fanaticism culminated into DAD

However, Mr. Gandhi would have interfered into the matter, would have negotiated with Mr. Janna and in worst case he would have been either requested British authority to maintain law and order or he would have goon unto fast until death – for which he was very much renounced. **But Mr. Gandhi did not do either of them ......why**?

India - which had been the homeland of Sanatan Hindu religion - was split into two countries India and Pakistan – and there was no one to advocate for a Hindu Nation. What in fact been the religion of Mr. Gandhi and his followers in the Indian National Congress?

Partition of India and liberation of Pakistan was to be decided by British Parliament for which a cabinet mission has already arrived in India.

1. Why there had been a massacre of Hindus? What was their fault?

2. Whether India was divided or not it was a game of Mr. Nehru and Mr. Jinnah how - those slaughtered innocent Hindu – were concerned with this game?

3. What the hell Mr. Non Violence was doing?

4. Whether Mr. Nehru was concerned at all?

**It must be observed that Calcutta Killing was the third episode of the series initiated in 1921.**

_The history of India's Partition is incomplete without a mention of the sordid episode of the Great Calcutta Killings of 1946 when Calcutta was overrun by the vicious forces of communal frenzy._

The resistance put up by the Hindus of all shades and origins was an archetype of selfless patriotism in defiance of a majority government and a repulsive political narrative. The offering of resistance by brave hearts like Mukhopadhyay, in the long run, prevented Calcutta and the whole of the eastern bank of the Ganges from getting engulfed by Pakistan.

### *The Build-up to the Direct Action Day*

The Cabinet Mission in India (1946) to arrange transfer of power from British rule to Indian leadership proposed an initial plan of the composition of the new Dominion of India and its government. However, this could not address the alternative plan to divide the country into a Hindu-majority India and a Muslim-majority Pakistan as proposed by the Muslim League.

The Muslim League planned a general strike *(herbal)* on 16 August terming it as Direct Action Day to protest this rejection, and to assert its demand for a separate Muslim homeland.

Muhammad Ali Jinnah said if the Muslims were not granted Pakistan, he would launch

"Direct Action". The Muslim League Council Meeting held during the period 27–29 July 1946 passed a resolution declaring that the Direct Action Day was intended to unfold direct action for the achievement of Pakistan.

*Jinnah gave enough indication of his evil intentions* – he said **he would have "India divided or India burned",** that the League had bidden **"goodbye to Constitutional methods"** and would **"create trouble".**

Syed Muhammad Usman, then Mayor of Calcutta, issued a widely circulated leaflet that said: *Kefir! Toder dhongsher aar deri nei! Sarbik hotyakando ghotbei!* (Infidels! Your end is not far away! You will be massacred!)

In order for the Islamist mayhem to go unchecked, Hindu officers were sent on leave and Pathan and Hindustani Muslim officers were appointed in their place at 22 out of 24 police headquarters of Bengal and in the majority of the police stations of Calcutta, by the then Bengal Prime Minister H.S. Suhrawardy. Many of those officials aided the Muslim Leaguers in raping and butchering Hindu women.

_**Killing of Hindus and Retaliatory Violence**_

The first instance of killing of Hindus was reported in Beliaghata in the early hours of 16 August, a *Jumma Baar* (Holy Friday). Two Bihari Gwalas (milkmen) were killed by Muslims. With inflammatory anti-Hindu slogans in their lips, soon after, shops, restaurants and cinema halls owned by Hindus were vandalised, looted and set on fire by Muslims.

Prime Minister Suhrawardy's speech in the League's Calcutta Maidan Rally may have meant an open invitation to disorder. Marauding Muslim gangs led by infamous criminals like Munna Chaudhary and Meena Punjabi started attacking Hindus and looting Hindu shops with brickbats and bottles as weapons.

Hindu men and boys were brutally massacred while girls were disrobed, abducted and raped. Many were taken as sex slaves. Golok Bihari Majumder, a senior police official had witnessed naked and deli bed Hindu girls hanging from a slaughterhouse in central Calcutta. Many Hindus went missing as their corpses were simply dumped into the Ganges or city canals.

The spate of destruction continued throughout the night of 16 August, up till the next day that witnessed one of the terrible massacres at Kesoram Cotton Mills in the slums of Lichubagan. 300 (400-600 according to some reports) Odia Hindu laborers were slaughtered at the hands of an Islamist band led by communist textiles union leader Syed Abdullah Farooqui and Elian Mistry, a hardliner.

According to conservative estimates, 7,000 Hindus were killed or went missing in the first two days. Estimates vary between 4,000 and 20,000. At this juncture, Gopal Chandra Mukhopadhyay also known as Gopal *Patha* (*Patha* means a male goat), *who* owned a meat shop in Calcutta emerged from the dregs of devastation. He hailed from a family of freedom fighters and was the nephew of the revolutionary, Anukulchandra Mukhopadhyay who was involved in the famous Rodda Company Arms Heist Case.

He was joined by Hindu men like Jugal Ghosh and Vijay Singh Nahar. Under the banner of his organization Bharat Jatiya Bahini, Mukhopadhyay organized thousands of Hindus and armed them with swords, pistols and lathis. Most of the arms and ammunition were provided by the Marwari traders who had purchased those as 'precautionary measure' from American soldiers, which were later used during the riot. Acid bombs were manufactured and stored in Hindu-owned factories before the outbreak.

Hundreds of Hindu volunteers of Vyayam Samitis (physical culture clubs) of Calcutta, Howrah and Hooghly and religious organizations like Arya Samaj acted as foot-soldiers of Hindu resistance. Punjabi Sikhs, Bihari Goalas and lower-caste Hindus of UP also contributed en masse to the muscle power.

Hindu Mahasabha and a section of the Congress and Forward Bloc put their manpower behind them. The figures of Muslim casualties were heavier as Hindu retaliation picked pace, and Muslims started leaving the city. Skirmishes and clashes between the communities continued for almost a week.

Finally, on 21 August, Bengal was put under Viceroy's rule. Battalions of British troops, supported by battalions of Indians and Gorkhas, were deployed in the city. The rioting reduced on 22 August. In these six days, thousands died in brutal conditions.

Methods of murder varied from stabbing, piercing, torching, bludgeoning, severing limbs, cutting, disemboweling to gagging, gassing, and throwing half-dead bodies in the water, and pushing the bodies into waste pipes and drain choking the latter. Bastis, already with infamous names such as Nakashipara, Karamtolli, Sahebbagan, became the most gruesome sites of murder.

Needless to say, had there been no Hindu resistance, the whole strip of land between

Bhagirathi-Hooghly River and present-day Indo-Bangladesh Border would have gone to Pakistan. The city of Calcutta would have been pushed into the fledgling Islamic state, even in the event of West Bengal becoming part of India. Why so? Let us examine the strip of land in question.

## *Failed Plan of Muslimising Calcutta*

A glance into the case of Calcutta City and the district of 24 Parganas would reveal the notorious motifs of the Muslim League. This is because there are recorded instances of the provincial government's plan to settle large numbers of Bihari and Hindustani Muslims in the Barrackpore industrial belt and in the rural and suburban areas and elsewhere for instance, in the southern fringes of Calcutta.

To substantiate this claim, Kalipada Biswas in his book *Jukto Banglar Shesh Odhyay* (Final Chapter of United Bengal) mentions that there are numerous evidences of settling large numbers of North Indian Muslims in Gumo and Habra regions in North 24 Parganas.

Had the Muslim fundamentalists emerged victorious in the Calcutta Pogrom, then within a year, they would have succeeded in altering the religious demography of the 24 Parganas district which was already 33 percent Muslim.

In the case of the provincial capital of Calcutta, the exchange of a letter dated 25 January 1947, between Raghib Ahsan of Bihar Muslim Relief Committee (Bengal) and Muhammad Ali Jinnah revealed the nefarious plan to settle 5 lakh Bihari Muslims in Calcutta. We find a similar mention of this plan in the autobiography of Sheikh Mujib, then a Muslim National Guard leader who later became the founding father of Bangladesh. When this letter was being exchanged, Bengal already had 3.5 million Muslim refugees from Bihar.

These Bihari Muslims were refugees who had to flee their home districts during the 1946 Bihar anti-Muslim riots. Ahsan, in his letter, urged Jinnah to direct the Bengal government to establish a 'Bihari Refugee Rehabilitation Department' and enact a 'Land Acquisition Law' for facilitating settlement of Muslims in large numbers in the city.

There were plans to nationalize the jute industry, which constituted the backbone of Calcutta's economy. The plan had ulterior motives. Ahsan wrote to Jinnah, *"Calcutta is the city of jute. Calcutta is the port of jute. Calcutta has been built by jute trade and industry and jute is 100 percent a Muslim monopoly product. But it is 100 percent exploited by Marwari-British capital through Bihar Hindu labor. **The moment the jute industry is nationalized, Calcutta will be Islamized.** Bihar* (Muslim) *refugees will be employed, and Bengal capital will be free from the Marwari pest."*

Henceforth the nationalization plan was equated to the 'Islamisation' of Calcutta. There were also plans at implementing a 50 percent Muslim communal ratio rule for all central government offices in Greater Calcutta Zone. There were 200 such establishments in the region. The plan stated envisaged that the Collector of Customs must be a Muslim, the Chairman of the Calcutta Port Trust must be a Muslim, and 50 percent of Railway coolies at Howrah, Sealdah, Kanchrapara, Asansol and Kharagpur must be Muslims.

Ahsan urged Jinnah to issue a directive to Suhrawardy to enforce 50 percent Muslim communal ratio rule in factories, firms, companies and mills and employ Bengali Muslims and Bihari Muslim refugees who would be settled in vacant Khas Mahal lands and lands of Calcutta Corporation and Improvement Trust. Bengal's transport sector (tramways, taxis, buses and steamers) was also to be nationalized in order to ease the communal reservation scheme for Muslim employees.

It must be noted here that in 1947, Calcutta Proper had a population of 21.09 lakh, of which more than 4.98 lakh were Muslims whose culture was Urdu-based. Of the remaining 16 lakh Hindus, nearly 5 lakh (32 percent) were Hindu migrant laborers from neighboring and far away provinces like Orissa, Bihar, UP and Punjab. Therefore, resident Hindus constituted roughly 11 lakh of the city's population.

Settling 5 lakh more Muslims in Calcutta would have taken their total population to somewhere around 10 lakh. That would have made the city 49 percent Muslim. Another 2-5 percent addition could have been provided by implementing the communal ratio rule by importing Bengali Muslims and few more Hindustani Muslims of the contiguous areas into the city.

There were incidents of persistent and sporadic tensions between Hindus and Muslims in the aftermath of the Killings of August 1946. In such a communally charged environment, there was a widespread notion among the Bengali Muslims that Bengal would be partitioned along the Bhagirathi-Hooghly River and that the city of Calcutta would be a part of East Pakistan.

When given an option of India or Pakistan, many Bengali Muslim government employees had written 'Pakistan, preferably Calcutta' in their opinion forms. This was no doubt a part and parcel of a conscious plan of altering the religious demography of the city.

The Muslim League had, from the very beginning, advocated for the inclusion of

Calcutta and its adjoining districts in Pakistan. When the Radcliffe exercise was in operation, the Bengal Governor Frederick Burrows proposed that Calcutta be excluded from both the Bengals and instead be administered by a 'council'. He feared there could be 'riots' in case Calcutta was handed to West Bengal.

Bhabatosh Dutt mentions that Muslim professors of Islamia College, Calcutta (now, Maulana Azad College) wrote in their opinion forms, 'Pakistan, preferably Calcutta'. One of them tried to console Dutt by saying, 'at least you are going to have Howrah'. However, even before the Radcliffe Award was out, it became clear that Calcutta was to remain in India.

### *A Strategic Victory for Bengali Hindus*

The Hindu retaliation in the Great Calcutta Killings strengthened the morale and self-determination of the Hindus of Bengal. It was becoming increasingly evident with every passing day that any attempt to truncate the Bengali Hindu homeland would be met with severe repercussions from the Bengali Hindu side. By then, the Hindus led by Syama Prasad

Mukherjee began politically organizing themselves for a fervent homeland movement.

Bengal's partition along the 400 km-long Hooghly River would have proven fatal to India in terms of national security. The Muslim League not only aspired to integrate Calcutta into Pakistan but also had plans to destroy the preeminent Howrah Bridge- the only connecting footbridge between eastern and western banks of the Ganges at that time. The merger of Murshidabad, the only Muslim-majority district, in Pakistan would have ensured Pakistani control over the Cossimbazar Port.

The stretch of land between Bhagirathi-Hooghly and Indo-Bangla Border comprises the eastern half of Murshidabad district; the whole of Nadia and 24 Parganas districts; and the city of Calcutta. In 1947, Murshidabad was a Muslim-majority district with Muslims constituting nearly 55 percent of the district's population. The district would have easily become a part of Pakistan in event of boundary demarcation. Murshidabad lied contiguous to East Bengal.

Murshidabad district that was dissected by Hooghly River was added to West Bengal only to keep the headwaters of Calcutta Port under Indian control. As evident, the Muslimisation of Calcutta Port Trust in compliance with the League's plans as stated earlier was directly related to the Pakistanization of Murshidabad. Soon, Pakistan would have dried up the Hooghly River by deviating river waters away to East Pakistan, resulting in a logistic and economic collapse of the Calcutta Port.

Nadia was also a Muslim-majority district in general. In particular, the eastern sub districts of Kushtia, Meherpur and Chuadanga were overwhelmingly Muslim whereas Krishnan agar and Ranaghat were Hindu-majority sub districts.

If the border was demarcated along the Hooghly River, then the Hindu claim to the Vaishnavite holy city of Nabadwip would have been preserved as it lay on the western bank. Nabadwip would have been part of India. However, it meant that two other Hindu holy cities that lay on its eastern bank: Shantipur and Mayapur succumbing to Pakistan's territorial engulfment.

It must be mentioned here, that the two Hindu-majority subdistricts of Nadia were placed in Pakistan on the eve of independence. The Hindus of Nadia agitated against this decision. There was a complete blackout observed throughout the subdistricts and Hindu women refused to lit ovens as a mark of protest. Three days later, the Hindu-majority areas were finally severed from Pakistan and placed in West Bengal. It goes without saying, the unwavering defiance shown by Nadia's Hindus, was wholly inspired by the Hindu resistance put up in August 1946.

However, the placing of Calcutta and adjoining districts in Pakistan implied a Hindu Bengal with a further reduced area (roughly 20 percent of undivided Bengal) with a huge burden of the population in the interior districts like Bardhaman, Bankura and Medinipur. The three districts to have absorbed three-fourth mass of East Pakistani Hindu refugees after Partition were: Calcutta, 24 Parganas and Nadia. A Partition along the Hooghly River may have complicated the transnational journey of the refugees.

The vast stretch of terrestrial porous border between the eastern bank and Indo-Bangla border facilitated their mass migration to India. Vast tracts of Nadia and 24 Parganas like Bangaon, Ranaghat, Barasat and Jadavpur are inhabited by the East Bengali Hindu refugees and their descendants till date.

Also, the shape of present-day northern West Bengal would have remained uncertain. If the eastern bank districts were placed in East Pakistan, it implied a significant reduction in the bargaining power of the Bengali Hindus in securing northern Bengal from the clutches of Pakistan.

The merger of Hindu-dominated regions like West Dinajpur and Maldaha would have remained a question mark. In absence of a merger, the southern districts would have remained totally cut-off from the northern districts like Jalpaiguri and Darjeeling.

In all probability, Calcutta would have been subjected to an unnatural referendum, given the options to join Pakistan or India. The Muslim League government could have easily shown those 5 lakh non-Bengali Hindus as 'migrants' thereby slashing them off electoral rolls. A demographic invasion by settling Muslims in the city would further outnumber the Bengali Hindu voters. India could have lost Calcutta forever, in event of a pro-Pakistan mandate.

The internal exchanges with regard to Calcutta's demographic exercise within the Muslim League happened in the aftermath of the Great Calcutta Killings. It is obvious that had the Muslim Leaguers emerged victorious out of it, then it would have easily facilitated capital city's integration into Pakistan.

Collating the Past with the Present

The gallant show of strength and organization acumen by the Hindus in 1946 is a facsimile for the Hindus of present-day West Bengal to emulate. A state that has been ruled by the communists and lately, the Trinamool, has abruptly eroded this glorious chapter from the pages of history. The successive political regimes have adhered to blatant Muslim appeasement. The Marxist rule in West Bengal has brushed the saga of Hindu defiance under the carpet.

The foremost criteria for the formation of the Bengali Hindu Homeland in 1947 were the substantial Hindu majority and security of Hindus. However, in present times, both have been under persistent attacks by Islamic fundamentalists. The numerous incidents of communal riots verify the claim. Time and again, protracted Islamist persecution has shrunk the Bengali Hindu Homeland.

Already, three districts have turned into Muslim majorities. A dialogue on Hindu persecution in the urban spaces of West Bengal is still regarded as a topsy turvy irrational subject. That is why the state remains susceptible to the danger of Islamism that is trying to wrest political control.

Those who cannot remember the past, as nineteenth-century Spanish philosopher George Santayana had famously said, are bound to repeat it.

Corpses lying in a cart on their way to be cremated after bloody rioting

Men adding wood & straw to funeral pyres in preparation for cremation of many corpses after bloody rioting.

## Chapter V

# *Noakhali   Hindu Genocide*

**QUIT NOAKHALI OR DIE, GANDHI WARNS HINDUS**

NEW DELHI, India, April 7 (AP) —Mohandas K. Gandhi, who has been attempting to insure communal peace in the Bengal and Bihar areas, said today religious strife in the troubled Noakhali section of Bengal seemed to call for Hindus to leave or perish "in the flames of fanaticism."

*"My heart bleeds, my brain is strained to think that the East Bengal Hindus who were in the vanguard in the struggle for freedom, will be deprived of their ancestral home and hearth."*

*"I do not want to die a discredited or a defeated man... I would rather die in Noakhali than go back a defeated man."*

Mr. M. K. Gandhi

*Mr. M. K. Gandhi was defeated.....in 4th round after sacrifice of innumerable Hindus. Great Non Violent Mahatma!*

xxxxxxxxxxx

It was Circa 70 when Jews became subject to religious persecution for the first time. Then ancient Roman Army destroyed Jerusalem, killed more than 1 million Jews, and forced almost 100,000 Jews to become slaves and captives. Tens of thousands of Jews from Palestine were also dispersed to other sites in the Roman Empire. This saga of persecution ended with holocaust or mass murder of Jews under the German Nazi regime from 1941 until 1945.Jews roamed across the globe for 2,000 years but none of such atrocities was disregarded ever. Each and every Jewish book expresses these as blackest days in their own history and the same concepts are transferred from one to the next generation. But we forget.

When it comes to main stream media Hindu projected as terrorist and Hindu organization projected as Hindu Taliban by India intelligentsia *but if we go through history what we say dark chapter which are even closed from memory of common mind and today most ancient civilization becomes terrorist in its own land*. It started well before India independence when riots broke out Chittagong Division of Bengal in October-November 1946 a year before Indian's independence from British rule. It affected the areas under the Ramganj, Begumganj, Raipur, Lakshmipur, Chhagalnaiya and Sandwip police stations in Noakhali district and the areas under Hajiganj, Faridganj, Chandpur, Laksham and Chauddagram police stations in Tipperah district, a total area of more than 2,000 square miles.

Massacre which started on 10 October, on the day of Kojagari Lakshmi Puja and continued unabated for about a week.

It is estimated that over 5000 Hindu were killed, hundreds of Hindu women were raped and thousands of Hindu men and women were forcibly converted to Islam. Around 50,000 to 75,000 survivors were sheltered in temporary relief camps in Comilla, Chandpur, Agartala and other places.

Apart from that around 50,000 Hindus remained marooned in the affected areas were under the strict surveillance of the Muslim hooligans.Noakhali genocide also known as Noakhali carnage was a series of massacres, rapes, abductions and forced conversions of Hindus and loot and arson of Hindu properties by Muslim community in the districts of Noakhali and Tipperah.

## Chronology

1. 29 August 1946 Anti-Hindu riots break out in Noakhali on the day of Id-ul-Fitr. Murder, loot and abduction of the Hindu population continue for a week.

2. 6 September 1946 Ghulam Sarwar Husseini formally joins the Muslim League.

3. 7 September 1946 Ghulam Sarwar Husseini addresses a huge Muslim crowd at Sahapur market, exhorting them avenge the Muslim deaths in the Great Calcutta Killings. He urges the Muslims to fabricate weapons and wield them on Hindus. A huge procession is taken out to mourn the Muslim lives lost in Calcutta.

4. 2 October 1946 Frequent instances of stray killings, snatching and looting start throughout the district of Noakhali.

5. 10 October 1946 N. G. Ray, the District Magistrate of Noakhali leaves Noakhali, two days before his scheduled departure on 12th. The large scale massacre of Hindu population commences. Surendranath Basu along the inmates and employees of the Narayanpur estate are massacred.

6. 12 October 1946 Eminent Hindu families, their relatives, dependants, servants and employees are massacred at Karpara, Gopairbag, Shayestanagar, Nandigram and Noakhali.

7. 19 October 1946 The British Indian Army is flown into Noakhali. The Army would take another week to reach the trouble spots and about a month to effectively rescue potential survivors.

8. 16 October 1946 Mc Inerney, the new District Magistrate of Noakhali, assumes charge. Huseyn Shaheed Suhrawardy acknowledges loot, plunder and forcible conversion of Hindus at a press conference in Kolkata, but downplays the mass killings, gang rapes and forcible marriages.

9. 22 October 1946 Ghulam Sarwar Husseini is arrested.

10.    7 November 1946 Mohandas Gandhi arrives in Noakhali for relief work.

11.    2 March 1947 Mohandas Gandhi leaves Noakhali.

12.    23 March 1947 Pakistan Day is celebrated in Khilpara in Noakhali district.

**Here are some excerpts.**

"Worst of all was the plight of women. Several of them had to watch their husbands being murdered and then be forcibly converted and married to some of those responsible for their death. Those women had a dead look. It was not despair, nothing as active as that. It was blackness.......the eating of beef and declaration of allegiance to Islam has been forced upon many thousands of as the price of their lives" – written by Miss Muriel Leister, member of a relief committee sent to Noakhali, on 6th November, 1946,(V.V. Nagarkar – Genesis – p 446).

**October 23, 1946 edition of Amrita Bazar Patrika stated clearly:**

"For the 13th day today, about 120 villages in Ramganj, Lakshmipur, Raipur, Begumganj and Senbag thanas (police stations) in Noakhali district with a Hindu population of 90,000 and nearby 70,000 villagers in Chandpur and Faridganj thanas in Tippera (Comilla) district remained besieged by hooligans. Death stares the people of these areas in their face and immediate rushing of supply to these areas with the help of military, which alone could do it, would save the lives of these people, most of whom have been without food for the last few days."

**On 16/10/1946, The Statesman reported:**
"In an area of about 200 sq miles the inhabitants surrounded by riotous mobs, are being massacred, their houses being burnt, their womenfolk being forcibly carried away and thousands being subjected to forcible conversion. Thousands of hooligans attacked the villages, compelled them (Hindus) to slaughter their cattle and eat. All places of worship in affected villages have been desecrated. The District Magistrate and the Police Superintendent of Noakhali took no step to prevent it."

Noakhali carnage took place due to several factors; one of them was the need of Muslim vengeance to defeat in Great Calcutta Killing by Hindus. On October 10, 1946 the pogrom started with the rabble-rousing speech of Gulam Sarwar, an ex-M.L.A of Muslim League at Begumganj Bazar. *A dreadful anti-Hindu speech by quoting verses of Quran exhorting Muslims to kill the Kafir and idolators and perform religious duty was given*. This was followed by violent assaults of Muslim mobs on Hindu properties, killings of hundreds of Hindus, rapes of Hindu women – a complete savagery.

**When the correspondent of 'Amrit Bazaar Patrika' S.L.Ghosh reached noakhali, he reported:**
"The horror of the Noakhali outrage is unique in modern history in that it was not a simple case of turbulent members of the majority community (Muslims) killing off helpless members of the minority Hindu community, but was one whose chief aim was mass conversion, accompanied by loot, arson and wholesale devastation... No section of the Hindu community has been spared, the wealthier classes being dealt with more

drastically. Abduction and outrage of Hindu women and forcible marriages were also resorted. The slogans used and the methods employed indicate that it was all part of a plan for the simultaneous establishment of Pakistan."

## Muriel Lester

Muriel Lester, a British relief worker in Noakhali, dew a pen picture of the plight of Hindu women during the genocide:

"Worst of all was the plight of women. Several of them had to watch their husbands being murdered and then be forcibly converted and married to some of those responsible for their death. Those women had a dead look. It was not despair, nothing as active as that. It was blackness... the eating of beef and declaration of allegiance to Islam has been forced upon many thousands of as the price of their lives."

## Jivatram Bhagwandas Kripalani

Describing the events in Noakhali, Jivatram Bhagwandas Kriplani, the **President-elect of the Indian National Congress said:**

"The attack on the Hindu population in the districts of Noakhali and Tipperah was previously arranged and prepared for and was the result of League propaganda – it was absolutely communal and one-sided; the authorities had warnings of what was coming beforehand; the Muslim officials connived at the preparations going on, and a few encouraged; the Police did not function during the riots, there being no orders to fire except in self-defense; there were a very few miscreants, if at all, from outside; and there have been many cases of forcible marriages and religious conversions en masse."

**On 21st October 1946, Kripalani observed:**
"I am clearly of opinion that whatever the Government, Provincial or Central, may or may not do, every Bengalee, male or female, has to defend him or herself by whatever means he or she can think."

**Sucheta Kripalani**
Sucheta Kripalani, the leader of Indian National Congress and wife of Jivatram Bhagwandas Kripalani and who later became the Chief Minister of Uttar Pradesh, the first woman to become a Chief Minister in India, lauded the bravery of **Rajendra Lal Roy Chowdhury in the following words:**
"Fortunately for the Hindus, Shiva ji and Guru Gobind Singh are not mythical figures buried in the dusty pages of learned

historical treatises; they are living forces inspiring our daily life. Their footsteps were followed in his humble and limited sphere by Rajendra Lal Roy Chowdhury, who died a martyr's death in his village home fighting almost single-handed against thousands of armed hooligans. His fight in defense of faith and family honor was, in Acharya Kripalani's significant words, 'the nearest approach to non-violence.'"

## Mohandas Karamchand Gandhi

On 18th October 1946, when the news of Noakhali reached Mohandas Gandhi through a telegram from Bidhan Chandra Roy, he commented:

"If one half of India's mankind was paralyzed, India could never really feel free. I would far rather see India's women trained to wield arms than that they should feel helpless."

Commenting on the uphill task before him in restoring peace in Noakhali, Gandhi said:

"I do not want to die a discredited or a defeated man... I would rather die in Noakhali than go back a defeated man."

## QUIT NOAKHALI OR DIE, GANDHI WARNS HINDUS

NEW DELHI, India, April 7 (AP) —Mohandas K. Gandhi, who has been attempting to insure communal peace in the Bengal and Bihar areas, said today religious strife in the troubled Noakhali section of Bengal seemed to call for Hindus to leave or perish "in the flames of fanaticism."

Regarding the inevitability of Hindu exodus, he commented:

"My heart bleeds, my brain is strained to think that the East Bengal Hindus who were in the vanguard in the struggle for freedom, will be deprived of their ancestral home and hearth."

**Frederick Burrows**

On 6th December 1946, a month after Mohandas Gandhi's arrival in Noakhali, Frederick Burrows put forward his views regarding the futility of Gandhi's peace mission:

"It will take a dozen Gandhi to make the Muslim leopard and the Hindu kid to lie down together again in that part of the world."Commenting on large scale abductions of Hindu women, Burrows could not hide his glee: "Large scale abduction of Hindu women (by Muslims) was quite natural since Hindu women were more handsome than Muslim women."

**E. S. Simpson**
Describing the devastation of the Haimchar market, Simpson commented:

"It looks like destroyed by a high power bomb."

**How many people were killed in Noakhali Genocide?**
There have been very few scholarly studies on Noakhali Genocide and there has been no objective study regarding the number of Hindus actually died in the Noakhali Genocide. However, it is generally accepted that around 5,000 Hindus died as a result of the mass killings. Contemporary press reports cite a figure of 5,000 or even more. The Muslim League controlled Bengal Government however tried to downplay the incident and deny the figures in the press, while certain Muslim League owned media denied the genocide all together. The official investigation reports were never published. The British colonial administration, in order to hide their administrative inefficacy, too downplayed the

incidents Dr. Sachi Ghosh Dastidar, who has researched extensively on the atrocities committed on the Hindus in East Pakistan and Bangladesh, has noted that the elderly people in Noakhali recalled that 5,000 to 10,000 Hindus were killed in the Noakhali Genocide. Bangladeshi scholar Salam Azad and Islamic scholar M. A. Khan both give a figure of 5,000.

## How many people were forcibly converted in Noakhali Genocide?

As with the number of dead, there is also no clear consensus about the number of Hindus forcibly converted. However, it is accepted that figure ran into thousands and probably into hundreds of thousands. Contemporary press reports mention a figure of around 150,000 as quoted by Bangladeshi scholar Salam Azad. According to Islamic scholar M. A. Khan, at least 95% of the approximately 400,000 Hindus of Noakhali were forcibly converted to Islam.

## Why there is no memorial for the victims of Noakhali Genocide?

The Noakhali Genocide was almost immediately followed by the Partition of India, within less than a year. The province of Bengal was partitioned and the eastern half, including the districts of Noakhali and Tipperah became Pakistan, the homeland for the Muslims of the sub-continent. The Bengali Hindus eastern Bengal was forced to leave Pakistan through subsequent pogroms and genocides, most notably in 1950 and 1964. The rehabilitation of millions of Bengali Hindu refugees became real challenge before the Government of West Bengal and India. The memoirs of Noakhali became suppressed in the saga of struggle for a new life.

## CHAPTER VI

# THE

# RIOT OF

# PARTITION

## *WE*

### *Background*

In August 1947, when independence was granted to the former imperial domain of British India, it was partitioned into two countries – India and Pakistan.

India had been the largest possession of the British and a subject of the British Crown since 1858, when the East India Company's reign had been brought to an end in the wake of the Uprising and Revolt of 1857 against the Company rule.

Attempts to grant self-rule to the Indians was heavily debated since the early 1900s in the public sphere, the early results of which were the Indian Councils Act of 1909 and the Government of India Act of 1919. In 1935, the Government of India Act constituted a number of provinces with their own legislatures where representatives were elected on the basis of a limited franchise. It was planned that British India would be granted dominion status, *i.e.* self-government supervised by the Crown. If a majority of the princely states chose to join the scheme, India would have a confederate structure with powerful provinces and princely states and a weak center in charge of defense, foreign relations and currency.

This scheme never came into effect because the majority of the princely states refused to accept the 1935 Act and become a part of the proposed dominion. Provincial elections were held in British India in 1937. When war was declared between Britain and Germany in 1939, the British government declared India's involvement in the war without consulting any Indian leaders. In protest against this unilateral decision-making by the British regarding Indian interests, the Congress Governments in the provinces resigned. They demanded full independence in return for Indian cooperation in the war. Under pressure from the American governments, the British sent the Cripps Mission to India in 1942 to secure full support and cooperation in the war against Germany by trying to negotiate better terms for transfer of power. But the pre-conditions of the Mission were not accepted by the Congress and the Muslim League, both of whom had different priorities and outcomes in mind. The failure of the Cripps Mission led to the Congress launching the Quit India Movement and demanding full independence from British rule. On the morning the Movement was to be launched, all Congress leaders were put behind bars where they were to remain until almost the end of war.

In 1945, the Labor Party came to power in Britain and pledged to grant independence to India. Their plan was developed on the basis of the 1935 Act. Elections were held in all the provinces of British India the results of which were that the Congress won in seven out of eleven provinces and the Muslim League won all the seats reserved for Muslims. In 1946, the British Government sent the Cabinet Mission to India to secure arrangements for a peaceful transfer of power. The Cabinet Mission proposed a confederation as previously detailed in the 1935 Act. It also proposed that provinces could group themselves into regions which would decide how power would be shared amongst them. Three regions were proposed, one comprising the <u>North West provinces of Punjab, Sindh, Baluchistan,</u> and the North West Frontier Province, the second comprising Madras, UP, Central Provinces, Bombay, Bihar & Orissa and the third comprising <u>Assam and Bengal.</u>

It was proposed that the provincial legislatures would elect representatives to a Constituent

Assembly which would frame the Constitution of independent India. Although the Congress rejected the proposal for an interim government, they decided to join the Constituent Assembly in order to help frame the Constitution of independent India.

Mohammed Ali Jinnah declared 16 August 1946 as Direct Action Day as a show of force of support from the Muslim community for a separate nation. Riots spread through the cities of Calcutta and Bombay resulting in the death of approximately 5000-10,000 people with 15,000 wounded. On 9 December 1946, the Muslim League which had earlier accepted the proposals of the Cabinet Mission now withdrew its support on the ground that there was no guarantee for proper safeguards of the rights of the Muslim minority in the Assembly.

The demand for a separate nation for Muslims had been raised by various Muslim leaders in the previous decades, most famously by Allama Iqbal at a Muslim League conference at Allahabad in 1930 where he articulated the idea of a Muslim nation within India. The term "Pak-Stan" had been coined by Choudhry Rahmat Ali in the 1930s while he was studying at Cambridge University. On 23 March 1940, at a meeting of the Muslim League in Lahore, Jinnah had endorsed such a demand, though without naming "Pakistan".

The proposal of the Muslim League resolution, to unite the Muslim majority provinces and carve out a separate nation was resisted by the Congress at the outset. At that time, an interim government was in charge with the Congress and Muslim League sharing ministries and Nehru acting as the de-facto Prime Minister. But soon the arrangement broke down and Lord Mountbatten put forth the proposal to partition India using the three regions as had been suggested by the Cabinet Mission.

The first Partition Scheme was outlined in April 1947. Jawaharlal Nehru was against the idea of Partition itself. The revised scheme was sent to London and came back with the approval of the British Cabinet. On June 4, the scheme to Partition India was announced by Mountbatten and endorsed in speeches by Nehru and Jinnah on the All India Radio.

The Partition scheme, as announced, was largely in line with the proposals of the Cabinet Mission. The North-West region comprising Punjab, Sindh, Baluchistan and the North West Frontier Province was as proposed by the Cabinet Mission. The Eastern region was redrawn without Assam or the North East provinces. East Bengal and the adjoining Sylhet district would be part of Pakistan. Partition came as a great shock to Mahatma Gandhi but the Congress leadership under Jawaharlal Nehru and Vallabh Bhai Patel had accepted the proposition. However, the question of the final boundary was still undecided. The two largest provinces Punjab and Bengal had only a marginal superiority of Muslims over Non-Muslims – 53% to 47%. It was decided; therefore that the two provinces would be divided down the middle and the electoral register would be used to apportion some districts to Pakistan and the others to India.

The drawing of the boundary proved to be extremely contentious causing fear, uncertainty and widespread death and destruction. Cyril Radcliffe, KC, a barrister from Lincoln's Inn, London was put in charge of drawing up the boundary with the help of local advisors in Punjab and Bengal.

The negotiations amongst the leaders proved a nightmare for the <u>thousands of families</u> who suddenly found themselves uprooted in a land they had inhabited for generations. Law and order broke down and there was large scale massacre and looting as families left their homeland to trudge across the new, arbitrarily drawn borders. Women were abducted, raped, mutilated and killed along with children, both born and unborn. Families abandoned their ancestral properties and crossed the borders, forced to find a new life as refugees. In the Punjab and Bengal, refugees moved from each side to the other, in search of safety. Many Muslim families left from UP and Bihar to end up as *Muhajirs* (refugees) in Karachi. The Hindus of Sindh arrived in Gujarat and Bombay.

The Partition of India was one of the most defining events in the history of the Indian subcontinent. With no accurate accounts of how many died or lost their homes, estimates suggest that perhaps up to 20 million people were affected by the Partition and somewhere between 200,000 – 1 million lost their lives. Yet, several decades after the event, there was a severe lacuna that no museum or memorial existed anywhere in the world to remember all those millions. It is their untold stories which the Partition Museum records and narrates.

## Punjab

In 1940, at the Lahore Session, the Muslim League had demanded the Partition of India to create a separate Muslim majority state in the north-west of India. In opposition to this demand, Sir Sikander Hayat Khan of the Unionist Party had forged links with the Sikhs and signed the Sikander - Baldev Singh Pact in March 1942. The pact provided for *Jhatka* meat in government institutions, the inclusion of Gurmukhi as a second language in schools and guaranteed 20 percent representation of the Sikh Community in the Executive Council supported by the Unionists. This was in strong opposition to Jinnah's demand for a Muslim state. However, the situation changed with the unexpected death of Sikander Hayat Khan in 1942.

The Unionists and the Sikhs were unable to sustain the alliance.

The Akalis drew up a scheme of Azad Punjab which encouraged the creation of a new province of Punjab. Master Tara Singh emphasized that the scheme was conceived to act as an effective counter to the demand of Partition.

In the Punjab elections held in 1946, the Muslim League had won the most number of seats but fell short of a majority. It failed to form a coalition government with any of the other parties, and a coalition government headed by the Punjab Unionist Party's Sir Khizr Hayat Tiwana came to power in Punjab.

In January-February 1947, the Muslim League called for Direct Action in the Punjab Province. This unnerved the Punjab Premier, Sir Khizr Hayat Khan Tiwana, whose coalition ministry included ministers from the Congress as well as Sikh Parties. The coalition fell on 2 March 1947.

On 3 March, Hindu and Sikh leaders met in Lahore where they vowed to oppose the establishment of Pakistan. On 4 March, Hindu and Sikh students came on the streets to protest. Communal clashes broke out in different parts of Lahore. By the evening of 4 March, communal violence broke out in Amritsar and on 5 March, in Multan and Rawalpindi. The governor, Sir Evan Jenkins, imposed Governor's Rule on 5 March 1947 after the League failed to convince him that it had a stable majority in the Punjab Assembly. Punjab remained under Governor's Rule until power was handed over to the Indian and Pakistani governments on August 14 and 15.

Lord Louis Mountbatten assumed the role of the last viceroy on 24 March 1947. He announced the Partition Plan on 3 June 1947, declaring that the British had decided to transfer power to the Indian and Pakistani governments by mid-August 1947. The announcement resulted in a further increase in violence as uncertainty over the future began the greatest forced migration in history. The Partition of Punjab proved to be one of the most violent acts in the history of humankind.

Between 15-17 Augusts, there was great confusion about the actual boundaries between India and Pakistan. It was widely believed that Gurdaspur District would be given to Pakistan. Consequently, Pakistan dispatched Mushtaq Ahmed Cheema as Deputy Commissioner of Gurdaspur and the Pakistan flag flew over Gurdaspur for those days. Many cities, including Lahore, remained uncertain of their fate.

On 17 August 1947, the Radcliffe Award was made public. Three *tehsils* of Gurdaspur district on the Eastern bank of the Ravi were given to India while Shakargarh on the Western bank went to Pakistan. Many found themselves on the wrong side of the border suddenly. Lahore was awarded to Pakistan. The mass migration that followed saw the death of millions and displacement of many more. Families were torn apart. People migrating by trains were massacred and butchered. Women were killed, abducted and raped. Many were killed by their own families to 'protect the family honor'. The tumultuous wave of migration largely ended by 1948, but the rebuilding of lives continued for decades.

## Bengal and Assam

The movement of people across the border took a different form in Bengal as compared to Punjab. West Bengal had 5 million Muslims in a total of 21 million, while East Bengal had 11 million Hindus in a total of 39 million, almost equal percentages of the minority communities. Initially, cross-border movement was limited, with more Hindus moving westwards than Muslims moving eastwards. The two governments came to an agreement about protecting minorities on each side in

April 1948 with the specific aim of preventing violence similar to that seen in Punjab from occurring in Bengal. The flow of migration further reduced. This was also due to a strong Pan-Bengali identity.

However, communal riots later triggered migration a few years after independence. Between February and April 1950, riots led to a million and a half people migrating; 850,000 Muslims moved eastwards, and 650,000 Hindus moved westwards. Nehru and Liaquat Ali decided to sign a revised agreement to protect minorities on both sides. But the atmosphere had deteriorated. Between April and July 1950, 1.2 million Hindus left East Pakistan and 600,000 Muslims from West Bengal moved eastwards.

Even beyond the riots, fear of discrimination against minorities also led to migration in the 1950s. The language movement of the 1950s made Bengali Hindus uneasy. The issuance of passports in 1952 led to the fear that the option of migration would not be available later. Incoming refugees also led to a scarcity of resources which prompted waves of migration. However, because a lot of migration in Bengal happened after 1947-48, this was viewed as economic migration by the government, reducing the official aid that displaced persons received.

In 1964-65, communal riots following tensions in Kashmir led to an increased flow of Hindus westwards. The final large-scale migration came in 1970-71 on the eve of the formation of Bangladesh.

Mountbatten's Partition plan, announced on 3 June 1947, provided for a referendum to be held in the Sylhet district to decide whether it should remain a part of the Indian province of Assam or become a part of East Pakistan. In a meeting of District Officers convened to decide the dates of the referendum, it was suggested that the first fortnight of July be avoided due to heavy flooding which would curtail the ability of people to reach the voting booths. The British Referendum Commissioner, however, argued that based on the date of final withdrawal there was no negotiation possible with regard to the dates. The Sylhet Referendum was therefore held on 6 July 1947 and the results favored a merger with Pakistan. Assam thus lost a wealthy district in terms of the thriving tea, lime and cement industries which in turn resulted in a serious loss of revenue.

Partition affected the politics and lives of the people in the North East in several ways. It physically separated them from the rest of the country save for a narrow passage commonly known as the Chicken's Neck, which is only 17 km wide at its narrowest. Partition disrupted the natural channel of reverie communication, and rail and road networks that provided connectivity to this area and had adverse effects on the economy of Assam. It was forced to exist as a landlocked province, as its natural outlet to the sea since 1904 through the port of Chittagong became a part of East Pakistan. The adverse impact of Partition was noted in the Census Report of 1951, which observed that 'the far-reaching effects of this loss will continue to be felt by Assam as well as India'.

Partition also affected the social and economic lives of the various tribal communities in the region. It disrupted the traditional links that tribal communities, such as the Khasis, Jantias and Garos, had with the East Pakistani districts of Sylhet and Mymensingh, leaving them split between India and Pakistan, based on their place of residence.

## Sindh

The experience of Partition in Sindh was different from that of other States. Sindh, unlike Punjab and Bengal, was not partitioned demographically, but rather the entire state went to Pakistan. The State experienced fewer cases of physical violence and more frequently, reports of looting, destruction and distress sale of property. In fact, when Acharya Kripalani, the Congress president visited Sindh three months after Partition, he noted the lack of communal fanaticism and the influence of Sufi and vedantic thoughts among the Sindhis which spread the message of tolerance. Sindhis did not migrate en masse to India in the months shortly after Partition.

However, by November 1947, with the arrival of a large numbers of refugees (*Muhajirs*) from Bihar and Bengal in Sindh, an atmosphere of fear unsettled the Hindus. These *Muhajirs* living in crowded refugee camps began to occupy the homes of the Hindu Sindhis. Two major incidents of violence in Hyderabad (Sindh) and Karachi on 17 December 1947 and 6 January 1948, respectively, triggered the decision of the Hindus to leave.

More than the violence, it was the loss of their homeland which had nurtured their culture for centuries that left a deep and lasting impact on the Hindu Sindhis who migrated to India. Partition left them not only without a home but also alienated them from their way of life. In an environment where survival was a major issue, with the well-off Sindhis helping those in more dire conditions, the nurturing of culture was not a priority.

During the first half of 1948, approximately 1,000,000 Sindhi Hindus migrated to India;

400,000 more remained in Sindh. Evacuation continued for three more years, and by 1951 very few Hindu families remained in Sindh – about a scant 150,000 to 200,000. That trickle of migration has continued over the years and remains a continuing process.

On the issue of Sindhi culture and the reconstruction of their lives post-Partition, Saaz Agrawal in her book, "Sindh — stories from a Vanished Homeland" writes, "The capricious river Indus ran through their lands and it changed course often. One day, you'd be by the river bank, the next, you'd be flooded. Their surroundings created a people prepared for change

# Chapter VII

## Tribute to a non violent mahatma?

### 1948  Massacre

### Maharashtra Brahmin Genocide – 8000 Killed

Mr. Gandhi was assassinated by one Maharastrian Brahmin and allegedly the followers of Mahatma Gandhi slaughtered more than 8000 Maharastrian Brahmins –

**as a tribute to a non violent mahatma?**

The man who is known to have killed Gandhi was Nathuram Godse, a Chitpavan Brahmin from Maharashtra. His aide was Narayan Apte, another Brahmin. Soon after the assassination of M. K. Gandhi on 30th January, 2948, the Chitpavan Brahmin community of Maharashtra became the target of unprecedented attack by the members of the Congress party and other anti Brahmin groups, apparently to avenge Gandhi's killings. The instant pogrom was indeed ironical, given that such a mass scale genocide of a community could be organized to avenge the killing of a man who advocated non-violence and peaceful means to achieve one's goal, that of freedom from British colonial rule. The followers of the advocate of 'non-violence' did not take much long to trash his so called ideology and went on a looting and killing spree of the Chitpavan Brahmins of Maharashtra with a skewed logic of an entire community being forced to bear the brunt of the deed of one of their own.

Estimates suggest that around 8000 Brahmins were killed but there are no records of how many were forced to flee leaving their home and hearth behind. Besides mindlessly butchering the Brahmins, looted and burnt down their homes, ransacked their shops and businesses, raped their women, rendering them homeless. One Anand Khatavkar narrated the trauma and tribulations of his family as it went down to rags from richer being the target of selective killing and property burning. His grandfather was one of the richest cloth merchants of Pune at that time, being the owner of 3 clothes stores but were compelled to sell off all property to reduce trading credits. The family could recover only in the 70s.

The destruction of life and property began in Godse's home base, Pune and spread like wildfire elsewhere. The worst affected districts were that of Satara and Kolhapur. The properties of Veer Vinayak Sawarkar were torched because they believed that he was a co-conspirator in Gandhi's killing and his brother, Dr. Narayan Rao Sawarkar was stoned. He subsequently succumbed to his injuries in October, 1949.

Though all records and images of the macabre killings of the Maharashtrian Brahmins, who are generally known to be Hindu nationalists, was destroyed, the nature of the attacks, as available from the accounts of the survivors, their descendants and other chroniclers, it is apparent that it was a premeditated one, which involved prior planning as all the Brahmin families were well identified and targeted – there was hardly any scope of error. The said pogrom was certainly not a 'riot' as it was made out to be, by a certain section of the Congress apologists and their logic of making an entire community accountable for the killing of Gandhi, is purely puerile. The fact that hundreds of bloodthirsty marauders could be gathered to carry out acts of plunder and killing in such a short period of time is mind boggling, given the fact that we are talking of an era when communication was not so fast as it is to this day. The very thought of it makes one wonder if the plunderers and terror mongers were aware of Gandhi's proposed killing on that date? It is just a thought. However, the pogrom, it is obvious, was executed solely with the purpose of terrorizing the Hindu nationalist Brahmins into submission and to discourage them from defiance, which would make the life of the ruling dispensation of the time much easier.

This Brahmin genocide remains, to date, one of the most suppressed atrocities on Brahmin Hindus. Brahmins were killed, Brahmin women were raped, shops and houses were set on fire, livelihoods destroyed, and many Brahmins forced to flee, to save their lives and future generations.

'It's written in "City, countryside and society in Maharashtra states" that in Audh state alone the barbarity spanned across 300 districts in all thirteen talukas. Maureen Patterson concluded that destruction was more cataclysmic in Satara, Kolhapur. The properties of Veer Savarkar were also swindled and torched by the perpetrators. *Dr. Narayana Rao Savarkar was stoned to death.*'

Narayana Rao Savarkar and his family were pelted with stones, as they tried to escape from their residence. He was gravely injured and eventually succumbed to his injuries on 19 Oct, 1949.

Estimates were that 8000 Brahmins were killed, with no record or estimate of how many were forced to flee.

Albeit there are no official reports on death toll, estimates suggest that 8,000 Brahmins were massacred i.e more than the casualties that occurred during 1984 riots. The news was published in local and international newspapers but has been obfuscated later. Much to the chagrin, Aryas who stand in solidarity with Sikhs have failed their brethren thanks to their deep-seated ignorance of history. Even Marathi Brahmins took little to no initiative to demand justice. Sambhaji brigade and their avaricious toadies heading Maratha agitation in a bid for reservations have to expiate Marathi Brahmins with due interest first.

"Angry mobs pillaged, burnt and looted the homes of hundreds of innocent Brahmin families, and many people were killed. All on the baseless assumption that all Brahmins were complicit in the assassination of the Father of the Nation."

May kindly be added....

Every aspect of this genocide points to it being a premeditated crime, targeting a religious community, namely, Maharashtrian Brahmins, who were known for being staunch Hindu nationalists. For mobs of hundreds to thousands suddenly attack Brahmins within such a short period of time would require great ingenuity and extraordinary means of communication, technologically not available at that period. These were not "riots" as often labeled, but a *planned genocide*, because it was spread over the entire geography of Maharashtra, not just one mohalla or city, using arson, which is not lying around in everyone's backyard every day. The "mobs" attacking Brahmins knew who they were, where they lived, and had the means to attack them.

"My family stands as a proof. My grandfather was among the richest merchant in Pune and was having 3 cloth stores then which were gutted in selective killing and property burning incidence. The family was instantaneously reduced to poverty and we had to sell-off all the properties to reduce the trading-credits. The family recovered out of the losses only by late 70's."

And also that

This is one of the genocides for which little information exists, once again, by ***design.*** It is otherwise impossible that a targeted massacre of a religious community is neither known, nor documented anywhere properly, except for firsthand accounts of those who suffered, and individuals who documented the massacre at the time of its occurrence. There is every reason to believe that ***all evidence of this genocide was destroyed, along with images and news clips.***

***Xxxxxxxxx***

# Chapter 8

# Gandhian Secularism

*Mahatma Gandhi is the father of Nation and then how those millions of innocent lives did not get any favor from him?* **This is the biggest question.**

Mr. Gandhi was a great nationalist Hindu saint and his Philosophy was based on principles of *"Truth and Non violence"* however *"Hindu-Muslim-Unity"* was the additional component in "Indian Edition of this Philosophy". Needless to say that Mr. Gandhi was a great nationalist as he left South Africa for gaining independence of India.

## *Change in Concept:*

We are living in IT age now and IT model of Modern India makes everyone concerned to relook into the matter afresh because the traditional model of the said history gives you the story of those days which was acceptable to the authorities.

You will find that Mr. Gandhi in person and Gandhian Secularism has been determining during the evolution of Independent India. Furthermore Gandhian Secularism has remained behind the proceeding of the state of India.

Let's review different aspects of Mr. Gandhi and Gandhian Secularism as both together do still mater for the state of India.

*Mahatma Gandhi*

# *The Hindu Saint:*

Mr. Gandhi – on arriving back from South Africa presented himself before Indian Population - as a rational citizen of India residing countryside. Please see the Photo of Mr. Gandhi - displayed below – and you will agree that this cannot be a photo of a man been educated in London nor of a man coming back from South Africa.

Mr. Gandhi presented in such gesture - to gain concern toward him – using the Mirroring Effect: a principle of Public Dealing. When a citizen of India will see his gesture he will find that he is watching himself in a mirror.

Gradually he changed his gesture till a mahatma evolved in his personality. Mr. Gandhi presented himself in gesture of a saint because India has been a country of sambas (swami) and saints and people do worship them. Mr. Gandhi expected that Indians must believe him and follow him blindly. Mr. Gandhi was very much successful in this venture because of basic instincts of Hindu. *Whole population of Hindu accepted him as a saint – does not matter whether Mr. Gandhi was really a saint or was posing like a Mahatma.* Mr. Gandhi was a vegetarian and used to offer his prayer in the evening regularly and strictly – and these features added to the qualities of Mahatma.

## *Hindu Saint*

*However, Mahatma is a term taken from Hindu Religion* where it means "a Great Soul". However Mahatma Gandhi

1) did not take any Dichasia from any Hindu Guru –but even then Mr. Gandhi was tan as a Hindu saint? People – in Hindu religion are known after name of their Guru as swami Vivekanand is known as disciple of Rama Krishna.

2) began to hold his prayer meetings in a Hindu temple in Bhangi Colony and **persisted in reading passages from the [Quran] as a part of the prayer in the Hindu temple in spite of the protest of the Hindu worshipers there.** *Of course he dare not read the [Gita] in the teeth of Muslim opposition. He knew what a terrible Muslim reaction would have been if he had done so.*

3) The "Mahatma Title' was conferred by Dr. Annie Besent Head of the theosophical society on the grounds which are not within limit of this book to discuss. Mr. Gandhi - in fact - was a mahatma by designation. **But Mr. Gandhi did not allow this reality to be published before Hindu population.**

4) Mr. Gandhi carried the *tag of Mahatma* and was interpreted by Hindu as a great soul been blessed with Spiritual Power. However, there is almost no example in which a person who has not taken Diksha nor he has ever meditated was been blessed by spiritual power.

5) To conclude Mr. Gandhi was a Mahatma by designation but was wrongly interpreted by Hindu community. This was because of his gesture which he himself has designed for him. and he concealed this secret.

**Whether he was really a mahatma or he was a Mahatma by designation – is impossible to answer.**

Mahatma evidenced altogether five Hindu Genocide which were in series and there was enough time to check it but he did not do it but even then he was projected as Mahatma. This was his total failure to check it.

## Story of Uprise of Islam in India

Hindu were been ruled by British shoulders and been slaughtered in their homeland by Islamic jihadi, there was no one actually to check this calamity and to take them out of it.

1. There had been a group of Muslim who consider themselves as descendents of Moguls and thus winner and ruler over

India. They claim this country is their native place not the motherland.

2. During 1857 independence war of India, those Muslim who were either shoulders of Bahadur Sah Zafar or were employee they fought the battle of 1857 against British Empire. Somehow Britishers took it as Muslims war and in reply they started slaughtering Muslim exclusively with the intention that no such person would survive who can stand in future and claim himself of being survivor of Mogul legacy.

3. That attack over Muslim was so lethal that Muslim decided to run underground to save their lives – until situation becomes favorable for them – and they migrated anyhow to Agra where colonies of Muslim were there which were faithful to British Raj.

4. Thus they started living off the scene bearing pain    of defeat and humiliation of 1857 in form of a boil on their heart. Muslim kept on nurturing that boil waiting for a favorable climate. To conclude The Muslim Community was like a mature volcano which was boiling to explode but even then they were living off the scene.

5. This volcano sensed a pre explosive stage when caliphate movement was knocking India in shape of caliphate movement. **The Khilafat movement was an uprise of Indian Muslims in support of the Islamic caliphate,** in the wake of World War I. _It was aimed at Islamic dominion over India, by destroying the British Empire, with support from the Ottoman Empire (which was eventually exterminated in late 1922)._

6. It must be noted here that Muslim fellow and specially the Muslim Leaders were not considering them as a part of India rather they considered themselves as a member of Islamic India under British Rule. The Khilafat Movement in India was led by the Ali brothers, i.e. Shaukat Ali, Mohammad Ali Jauhar and Abul Kalam Azad and that volcano burst worst with the collaboration of Mahatma Gandhi.

7. **This is very confusing to find out those grounds over which Mr. Gandhi extended his support to Khilafat movement.** Some of the authors – being annoyed - went a step ahead to scribe **"Whom side Gandhi was?"** and a few dared to requisite "will the real Gandhi

stand              up              please".
https://timesofindia.indiatimes.com/coro
navirus

8. It was a mere speculation of Mr. Gandhi that Muslim community including their leadership will join hand in protest against British Empire seeking Independence – if he supports Khilafat movement. Such of his speculation led him to appease Muslim leaders beyond all limits.

9. Thus Mr. Gandhi provided an impetus to Khilafat movement and brought the Muslim community from off the scene to a level of being "accepted, appreciated and appeased by Hindu of India and their leadership" Mahatma Gandhi virtually provided all the nutrients and supplements to the Muslim league and supported it to bring Muslim League to the level of congress from where they went beyond congress because of their Militant power.

10.    Needless to say that Mahatma Gandhi did not mind militancy of Muslim League rather conferred the honor of "Quid-e- Azam" to Mr. Zinna but compelled to remain nonviolent and dependent on British support only

................and also he compelled Hindu by his non violent drive to remain helpless before armed enemy of Muslim League. Below are the observations in support

11.    Support of Gandhi and also of Congress party to the Muslim Caliphate movement according to policy of appeasement did not obtain the desired result he had intended. He had hoped to entice the Muslim leaders into embracing unity through openness, but they refused to integrate and maintained the "Khalifat Committee" as a separate and distinct element:

12.    The Muslims ran the Khalifat Committee as a distinct political religious organisation and throughout maintained it as a separate entity from the Congress; and very soon the Mapilla Rebellion showed that the Muslims had not the slightest of national unity . . . There followed as usual in such cases, a huge slaughter of the Hindus, numerous forcible conversions, rape and arson.

13.    This modus operendi provided a wide network of interconnected pipelines – build up by Muslim leaders at the behest of Non cooperation network

through which explosives could be pushed to destroy the piece of land. **When Muslim leadership succeeded in**

 a. **building that network and**
 b. **Procuring support, weapons and massacre exported invaded India**

That Islamic Volcano got blast on surface of Mallabar district and caused

14.  Mapilla Massacre *the Mapillla Rebellion as it was called was the most prolonged and concentrated attack on the Hindu religion, Hindu honour, Hindu life, and Hindu property; hundreds of Hindus were forcibly converted to Islam. Women were outraged.*

15. **The Mahatma who had brought about all this calamity on India** by his communal policy kept mum. He never uttered a single word of reproach against the aggressors nor did he allow the Congress to take any active steps whereby repetition of such outrages could be prevented.

16.  *On the other hand he kept on denying the numerous cases of forcend conversions in Malabar and Gandhi published   in his paper* **Young India'** *where he willfully and deliberately denied the huge number of forced conversion of Hindus there and declared that only one case of forced conversion*  ------

17. *Mr. Gandhi – in his paper* **Young India** published as "one case of forced conversion was observed in Malabar district" and knowingly denied huge numbers of forced conversion. Such act of Mr. Gandhi disqualify him as a man of integrity.

18. **His own Muslim friends informed him that he was wrong and that the forcible conversions were numerous in Malabar.** *He never corrected his mistake but went to the absurd length of starting a relief fund for the Moplahs instead of their victims*

19. After the Khilafat movement began to fade, communal tension brewing underneath the facade of 'Hindu-Muslim unity' surfaced. On the fateful days of **September 9th and 10th of 1924,** radical Islamist mobs unleashed the carnage was pre-meditated venture and resulted in the **exodus of the entire Hindu population from the area. The entire Hindu population** of Kohat was wiped out, forcing a further demographic change in favor of the Muslims. **the true face of 'Islamic fundamentalism' was exposed.**

20. It must be noted here that In between the onset of Mapilla massacre and that of Kohat was duration of three years during which it would have been ruled out if the Hindu leadership wanted so. ..................but this could not happen. Besides, Muslim league was been granted a

22 year long enough time to change the demography of Bengal and orchestrate the Great Calcutta Killing.

21. In 1946 or there about the Muslim atrocities perpetrated on the Hindus under the Government patronage of Surhawardy in Noakhali,. when Gandhiji had come forward to shield that very Surhawardy and began to style him as *'Sahib Saheb—a Martyr Soul (!) even in his prayer meetings.*

22. Not only that but Gandhiji began to hold his prayer meetings in a Hindu temple in Bhangi Colony and persisted in reading passages from the [Quran] as a part of the prayer in the Hindu temple in spite of the protest of the Hindu worshipers there. *Of course he dare not read the [Gita] in the teeth of Muslim opposition. He knew what a terrible Muslim reaction would have been if he had done so.*

23. The situation continued to disintegrate within the country under Gandhi "but like the proverbial gambler, Gandhiji continued to increase his stake [s]," by embracing the policies those   which would have been lethal to the Nation and on the is basis few of the authors called him a traitor.

**End of the Book**

Made in the USA
Columbia, SC
08 September 2024

41899665R00089